IMAGES OF ENGLAND

WESTHOUGHTON

The clock tower is the main feature of the Town Hall, and Market Street is the heart of the town. In February 1938, the clock was undergoing repairs, so it was possible to look back through time, at a murky Market Street, with the other main feature of the town, Saint Bartholomew's church, in the background. The bell was removed in January 1947, as the vibration was affecting the terracotta work. It didn't ring throughout the war years and was also considered unnecessary 'now that Big Ben booms out every night, and there are few people without a radio'. (photograph courtesy of *Horwich and Westhoughton Journal*)

IMAGES OF ENGLAND

WESTHOUGHTON

KEN BEEVERS

Market Street, c. 1950

Dedicated to Howfeners everywhere

First published in 2000 by Tempus Publishing
Reprinted 2001, 2004

Reprinted in 2008 by
The History Press,
The Mill, Brimscombe Port,
Stroud, Gloucestershire, GL5 2QG
www.thehistorypress.co.uk

Reprinted 2013

British Library Cataloguing in Publication Data.
A catalogue record for this book is available from the British Library.

ISBN 978 0 7524 1606 9

Typesetting and origination by
Tempus Publishing Limited.
Printed and bound in Great Britain by
Marston Book Services Limited, Didcot

Contents

Westhoughton Town Hall, and *Bolton Evening News* and *Horwich and Westhoughton Journal* offices, at No. 22 Market Street, in January 1937. The offices were opened in October 1926, and closed in June 1979. (photograph courtesy of *Horwich and Westhoughton Journal*)

Acknowledgements

This book would not have been possible without Bolton Libraries' policy to acquire and conserve photographs. The Library Service would welcome the opportunity to increase its photograph collection of the area. Photographs loaned to us can be copied quickly and returned to their owners.

I would like to thank Brian Clare, Eric Holt, Alan Davies, colleagues at Westhoughton Library, Bolton Archives and Local Studies Library, Bolton Museum, Christine Bell of the *Bolton Evening News* library, as well as members of the Westhoughton Local History Group, and Erna Naughton for permission to include excerpts from the work of Bill Naughton.

My thanks to the *Bolton Evening News* for permission to reproduce photographs from the *Horwich and Westhoughton Journal*.

'Don't miss the Bolton Evening News *for Looking Back,*
the best coverage of your town in years gone by.'

Introduction

This book is not a history of Westhoughton but a glimpse into its recent past using photographs from the Westhoughton Library collection. For those who wish to find out more, there is a comprehensive collection of material relating to the area in the library. The *Horwich and Westhoughton Journal* is a useful source of information and the Westhoughton Local History Group have contributed a great deal to what we know about the town, and have enriched the local studies collection with their work.

There are in fact few remains of Westhoughton's early history, but the name Westhoughton first appeared as 'Westhalcton' in 1240 and as 'Westhalghton' in 1327, being the Old English '*halh*' (haugh), meaning level ground by the side of a stream, and '*tun*', a village or hamlet. The prefix 'West' was added perhaps to distinguish it from other Haughtons in the area, possibly Little Haughton, in Swinton, a place now relatively unknown. Westhoughton lies on the old Roman road from Manchester to Coccium (Blackrod), the route followed by the A6, but was not an important settlement. In the Middle Ages the town was governed by monks from Cockersand Abbey, land having been granted to the Abbot by Thomas of Halcton, but the Abbey was far enough away for the people to retain their independence

From the sixteenth century, industry and agriculture existed side by side. In 1751 six out of fourteen of Squire Hulton's farms were worked by tenants, describing themselves not as farmers but as weavers or nailers. Coal was first worked in 1540 with small pits all over the district until larger pits opened in the middle of the nineteenth century. Throughout the seventeenth and eighteenth centuries there was an increase in the population and in manufacturing. The town had a skilled workforce and a ready source of power and could have been in the forefront of the development of the textile industry. One of the first power loom mills in the world was built in the town but this was destroyed by the Luddites in 1812, severely holding back the town's progress for many years, as no one wanted to invest. The population stagnated, trade declined and there was bitter hardship in the town. Only after silk weaving was introduced in 1826 did some prosperity return. By 1851 there were 500 weavers – this was a cottage industry that suited the people and their independent spirit. Cotton weaving was re-established on a large scale, which together with coal mining were the main industries.

In 1921 55% of the male resident working population were employed in coal mining. The pits though were closed one by one, the last one in 1936. With four million men out of work and six million living on the dole, Westhoughton was as badly affected as anywhere. In 1933 it was said that Westhoughton couldn't stand another six years of these losses without becoming an industrially derelict town. In 1934 'back to the land' was the recommendation to cope with the depression, for despite the mines and the industry it always had the air of a market town, a place where you could see the pithead next to the wheatfield. Rhys Davies, the town's MP campaigned for the area to have special status, doing all he could to help the town in its plight, in particular its 'necessitous children'.

The fact that it was once a colliery community, or a number of such communities, has contributed to the character of the town and helped shape the nature of its people. The experience of working as a miner, the hard work, working conditions, danger and acquaintance with tragedy, as well as the camaraderie, 'produced human beings familiar with areas of human experience seldom known by the average man', and gave colliery communities a character of their own. People were familiar with adversity, but had the spirit to overcome it. Given the background of unemployment and reliance on coal and textiles, the proposal in 1963 to create a 'new town' in conjunction with Manchester would have brought new industries, opportunities and facilities. Westhoughton though would have lost its own identity and character, and as a result the townspeople were against it. It would have been a very different town if the plans had gone ahead. This sense of independence goes back a long way. In 1924 the Mayor of Bolton, opening the new tram link, said that in the past the people of Westhoughton and Bolton looked upon each other as foreigners, and he hoped that the new service between the two would improve relations.

One of the traditions which gave Westhoughton its unique character in the past was the 'keaw yed' legend and wakes festival. Mottoes like the one on the Westhoughton Cricket Club noticeboard, which says 'Well its yon mons keaw, but! It's ma' gate-so?' and illustrations of the legend keep the story going. The festival though goes back a lot further than the story of the farmer and the gate. Poets and performers such as Brian Clare, Eric Holt and Ernie Ford preserve the dialect and traditions, and of course the Houghton Weavers are from the town. Indicative of this tradition is the fact that the Westhoughton Folk Club was voted Folk Club of the year in the BBC Folk Awards 2000.

Westhoughton has grown in recent years with several new housing developments and most people have to now travel outside the town to work. No doubt they don't think of the people of Bolton as outright foreigners anymore but that spirit of independence and unique character, illustrated in this book, is still there.

Ken Beevers
July 2000

Cows are a symbol of Westhoughton, and the cow's head in the above photograph was once prominent above *the Horwich and Westhoughton Journal* offices at No. 22 Market Street, but is no longer visible. There are four cows heads engraved on the belfry of the parish church of Saint Bartholomew, each one facing in a different direction, and they are incorporated in various associations with the town. The religious connection is that Saint Bartholomew is the patron saint of tanners and all who work in skins, and his emblem in art is the butchers' knife. This animal has led to natives of Westhoughton, 'Howfeners', being also known as 'Keaw Yeds', and there is more than one explanation for this. The adjoining shop still has a matching piece of stonework, with a portrait of Queen Victoria and the inscription, '1897 Diamond Jubilee Buildings', and the name of the sculptor, 'Harris'. (photograph courtesy of *Horwich and Westhoughton Journal*)

One

Civic Pride

'Wonderful Howfen'

Westhoughton Council, 1897-1898. From left to right, back row: Fred Hampson, manufacturer and rope maker (a steady, industrious and plodding man), James Bond, (insurance agent), Dr Tyndall, Percy Marsh, (barrister), Joseph Rothwell, (lived at The Laburnums, Clough Fold), John Fletcher, (fireman and socialist), Jacob Gill, (miner at Swan Lane colliery), W.E. Tonge. Front row: George Croston, (grocer and baker of Daisy Hill), James Lambert, (surface manager, Hulton Collieries), Thomas Partington (clerk), Arthur Leach, Roger Walker, (farmer), James Hartley (school attendance officer, and nuisance inspector). Full biographical details of these men are available in *Westhoughton Historic Review* by J. Clough, 1897.

Old Council Offices. The Westhoughton Local Board was formed on 2 December 1872, and met in a temporary building in Market Street, becoming an Urban District Council on 17 December 1894. The offices stood on land where Market Street adjoins Wilbraham Street. Ernest Bootle Wilbraham leased the garden opposite Sunny Bank to Peter Ditchfield in 1865 for 999 years at an annual rent of £7 2s 8d.

The laying of the foundation stones for the Town Hall, 18 April 1903, at 3 p.m. Needing larger accommodation, plans were made for a new building, and two stones were laid, one by Mr Roger Walker, the senior member of the council, and the other by the chairman, Mr W.E. Tonge. Mr Walker had been on the council since joining the Local Board in 1876 and was a farmer at Hart Common. He was an out and out Conservative, and member of the Episcopal Church. Mr Tonge was only thirty-six in 1903, and was the son of James Tonge, and member of a family which had long associations with mining. A Liberal, he worked for Hulton Collieries, and in 1894 was captain of Westhoughton Cricket Club when they won the Bolton and District League championship.

The Town Hall under construction in 1904. The architects were Messrs Bradshaw and Gass of Bolton, and the hall is built in the classic renaissance style, of red Ruabon terracotta. There was apparently a spot of bother about the clock, for the committee disliked the dials which were sent, and requested others that were entirely plain and free from visible ironwork. The new offices were opened by the chairman, Mr S. Taylor, on 7 December 1904, after a procession from the old offices led by a joint band from members of the Wingates and Westhoughton bands. Luncheon in the assembly rooms followed, rounded off with 'council pudding' and a programme of entertainment featuring artistes including Masters Tony and Terry Wilson, humorous duettists.

Westhoughton Library, and Carnegie Hall were built thanks to a grant of £3,500 from the Scottish philanthropist Andrew Carnegie. The building was formally opened on 24 March 1906 by George Grundy, Esq. JP, chairman of the council, but the reading room was not opened until May, and the lending of books, on which £300 had been spent, did not start until August. The first librarian was J.C. Scott, who retired in 1943. He organized a regular course of lectures for many years and these met with varying degrees of success. On the night of 7 November 1928, the lecture was by Chief Os-Ke-Non-Ton, a Red Indian Chief and Mohawk singer. In the full ceremonial costume of the tribal head, he told stories, donned the headdress of the medicine man, sang songs of the Indian on the warpath and showed how to kindle a fire by friction. Apparently the attendance was a record and 'must have rejoiced the hearts of a suffering Library Sub-Committee.'

The library on 3 December 1970. Use increased from the opening day in 1906 but it became increasingly popular after the open access system was introduced in 1930. It was reported that from that time, when readers were given free rein to browse at the shelves, 'borrowers visited in crowds'. Unemployment was also a significant factor in Westhoughton's increased interest in reading. During the strikes and cotton disputes the library reading room was besieged by visitors. It soon proved to be too small and by 1970 was so cramped that 'on Saturdays it was virtually impossible for two people to stand together to choose a book.' The room was completely rebuilt and doubled in size during 1971-1972, at a cost of £79,000. Chief librarians after Mr Scott, were Ann Stone, 1943-1955, Alice Wallwork, 1955-1958, Harry Hibbert, 1958-1973 and Dr Tom Dunne, 1973-1974, who was also deputy from 1969. One library assistant, Ada Bellis, worked with every chief librarian, retiring in 1969 after forty-eight years service. Librarians since local government reorganization have been Judith Smith, 1974-1994, Margaret Walsh 1994-1996, and Pat Ramsden. (*Horwich and Westhoughton Journal*)

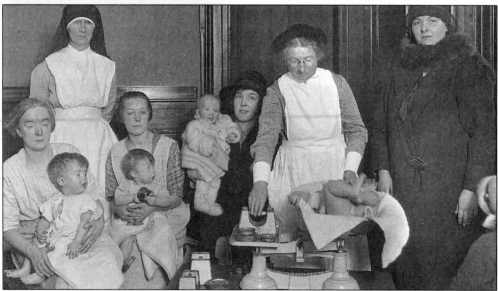

The clinic, 1928. Nurse Moore is on the left. The council purchased Sunny Bank, adjacent to the cenotaph, and furnished it as a maternity and child welfare centre and school clinic, as part of the memorial to men killed in the First World War. The clinic was open on 2 afternoons a week for mothers and children. Conditions were improving, and the death rate of children under 1 years old (per 1000) was decreasing. In 1923 the figure was 103, by 1924 it was down to 83, the lowest on record in the district. (photograph courtesy of *Horwich and Westhoughton Journal*)

The clinic, 1928. Home visiting had been improved with children being visited as early as possible after birth, with advice given on feeding, clothing, and general hygienic conditions affecting the child. In the Hart Common area there had been a serious outbreak of measles. Other factors affecting health were low wages, and an acute shortage of housing, with some shocking cases of overcrowding. (photograph courtesy of *Horwich and Westhoughton Journal*)

Mothers leaving Westhoughton Welfare Centre in February 1948, after having children immunised against diphtheria by Dr Taylor, Westhoughton's Medical Officer of Health. Among them were Mrs J. Bateson, of No. 339 Manchester Road, and her 10 months old daughter. The old prejudice against immunisation was gradually changing, as medical science opened a sure and safe way to protect every child from the dread disease. However by 1950, Dr Taylor was very concerned about smallpox, as out of 197 live births in Westhoughton in 1949, only 3 babies were vaccinated. In the same report Dr Taylor, echoing Dr Leigh in 1925, said that the acute housing shortage was a subject of paramount importance. Westhoughton's population in 1949 was 14,940 and, although in that year 63 council and 3 private houses were built, there were still 494 names on the housing waiting list, and approximately 321 of the applicants were living in lodgings. (photograph courtesy of *Horwich and Westhoughton Journal*)

Chorley Road, 1935. In 1935 these houses were considered by the council to be 'unfit for human habitation', in their submission to the Minister of Health. The clearance order was part of the council's proposals to deal with slum property under the Housing Act of 1930. At the enquiry in October 1935, Cllr Cowburn denied that much of the property under review could be classed as slum property.

Bolton Road, 1935. Comprehensive schemes of reconditioning were put forward by the owners, and as a result some houses were saved. Cllr Cowburn had strong views on compulsory slum clearance. 'I venture to say that there is no man in this country today who ever thought he would have to see an English Act of Parliament which robbed owners of their property without any compensation except just a 'mite', that might pay for demolition expenses.'

The rear of Nos 80-88 Dobb Brow, 1935. These cottages were saved from demolition, subject to the owners carrying out improvements. Dobb Brow derives its name from John Dobb, who could be claimed to be Westhoughton's first town planner. He was in possession of the farm, two cottages, and the Dobb Brow well, which supplied good drinking water. He let out plots of land in 1777 for building. His successor was John Hodkinson, who did more than anyone to develop the village. He built and sold cottages until 1882, when he disposed of the farm and most of the cottages to Richard Latham, a Lostock farmer. In 1935, at least three of his descendants were owner-occupiers. Many of the early tenants were handloom weavers and smallholders. The 1861 census lists seventeen handloom silk weavers, five handloom cotton weavers, three platelayers, and five farmers. The council said thirty of the houses were unfit but only a dozen had to come down.

The front of No. 19, and the rear of Nos 17, 21, and 23 Dobb Brow, 1935. Number 17 was to be demolished to allow the renovation of No. 19, and the Minister of Health agreed to Nos 21 and 23 being converted to one house. In defending the condition of the houses, evidence of the good health and longevity of the residents was presented. For example, one of John Hodkinson's tenants had made his own coffin, and although his house was below ground level on one side, he lived to a ripe old age. When very old he would often sleep in his coffin, and having come to the conclusion he would live for ever, sent for the late Roger Walker, farmer and Local Board member, to bring his gun! Another tenant, an old lady of seventy-eight, having recovered from a major operation was doing her own housework and looked like living as long as the old man referred to above. These cases were quoted to show the type of person Dobb Brow has produced. '*And they say these houses are unfit for humans.*'

Cemetery Street, 1935. As part of the clearance area, these cottages, at the end of the street were also known as Breaktemper. On the corner of Cemetery Street was a confectionery shop owned by Cllr Peter Scholes, JP.

The owner, desirous of a more pleasant name than Cemetery Street, called it Sunlight Valley, but no one else did!

Pendlebury Fold, 1935, was condemned by the council. It was situated between a small railway line to the Hulton Brick Works and the railway line from Bolton to Chequerbent. There are no longer any houses in Pendlebury Fold and the railway line has long gone, but there is a concrete works in the same location as the brick works.

Wingates Square, 1935. In 1886 the *Bolton Chronicle* reported that nine ancient cottages were unoccupied and dangerous. A youth playing in one of them was killed when the property collapsed. Two years later on 9 June a boy named Richard Foster was killed by part of the property collapsing. In 1892 there was a sale of farming stock at Wingates Square Farm by Henry Swindley, who was 'declining farming'.

Broadwalk. The first 230 homes on Hindley's estate were completed in 1922, with 300 more houses, including shops, added after the Second World War. The first of these houses to be completed were at Southfield Drive, the keys being handed over to the first two tenants on 20 June 1947. Delays in construction were due to the severe winter and material shortages. New houses were also built in Daisy Hill after the end of the war. Despite Dr Taylor's concern for the effect that the town's acute housing shortage was having on health, the council were hampered by the fact that the Ministry made the provision that only houses for mining and agricultural workers could be erected. There were complaints, but Cllr West, the vice-chairman of housing who opened the estate in October 1948, said that 'half a loaf was better than none'. Mr and Mrs Harper and Mrs E. Clearly received the keys to the first two houses to be tenanted by persons on the mining and agricultural waiting list. Future policy was to build more houses in Leigh Road, and plans for 900 homes were made.

Broadwalk, June 1948. Communities were close-knit and got together regularly to celebrate, and provide their own entertainment. A street party for the May Queen was held in June 1948. The Queen was Mary Ince.

The first steamroller acquired by Westhoughton Council, 1899. James Lee of Manchester Road was the driver.

Westhoughton's first ambulance, 1896. George Caldwell is in the centre. Westhoughton was not a particularly healthy place and an unusually healthy period led the newspaper to declare, 'It may be 'cowd Howfen' but it's been a very healthy one lately, when the death rate is 0.00 per thousand as it was last week. There looks a lot of figures about it but they don't come to much, and this week I am told there have only been two deaths, so that if things go on in this way the Local Board will have to set about advertising Westhoughton as a health resort.' (From *The Westhoughton and Hindley Times*, May 1884.)

In November 1947 the council were encouraging recycling – 'Salvage can help to relieve the rates'. Westhoughton Council employees are bundling paper and sorting bottles and jars, collected during the week by the cleansing department. Every month the council is able to dispatch about 9 tons of waste paper, 300 dozen bottles and jars, textiles, scrap metal etc. to an average value of about £80. This figure, it was said, could be improved with more complete co-operation from the general public. Far too much paper, for instance, was finding its way through dustbins to the tip. (photograph courtesy of *Horwich and Westhoughton Journal*)

Children waiting to cheer King George VI and Queen Elizabeth, who visited Westhoughton for thirty-four minutes on Friday 20 May 1938 on their tour of Lancashire. They passed over the boundary from Wigan at 12.17 p.m. and left via the Farnworth boundary, at 12.51 p.m. It was not an official visit so they only stopped briefly at the Town Hall long enough to receive the Mayor and Mayoress, and other important dignitaries of the town. Mills and shops closed early so that staff could see the procession. Six Westhoughton representatives were presented to the King and Queen at Bolton and the *Journal* described what the ladies were wearing. Mrs Dickinson, wife of the clerk to Westhoughton Council, 'wore a black and grey floral ninon frock under a black wool georgette coat and a black straw hat trimmed with an aigrette.'(photograph courtesy of *Horwich and Westhoughton Journal*)

The Royal car passes slowly by the White Horse on Market Street, where the crowd was several deep. There were two designated slow sections, with a maximum speed of 20mph. These were from Hewlett Street to Hart Common Post Office, and from Allenby Mill, Market Street, Bolton Road, to the White Horse. The start of each slow section was marked by a red flag and the end by a green flag. Dog owners were recommended to keep their dogs on chains to avoid the risk of being scared by the crowds. A radio car on the old mill ground kept in touch with police overhead in a light aircraft. (photograph courtesy of Brian Clare).

Some of the employees of Wigglesworth's Ltd with their Coronation decorations. Coronation festivities in Westhoughton were as follows; Friday 29 May, crowning of Coronation Queen (Alice Hobson of Taylor and Hartley's mill) and Charity Cup rugby final. Saturday 30 May, judging of the shop window competition, and Coronation parties. Sunday 31 May, called Coronation Sunday, had church processions. Monday 1 June was the Coronation Ball held at the Town Hall, and at Westhoughton Greyhound Stadium there were the Coronation Finals for 20 guineas and a trophy. Tuesday 2 June was Coronation Day – the procession assembles at Broadwalk 2.30 p.m. to leave at 3.00 p.m; there were prizes for fancy dress, children's advertising character, tableaux, decorated cars and cycles and events on the field. Wednesday 3 June, was the school sports day and ball at Daisy Hill. Friday 5 June the Coronation Dance at Carnegie Hall. Saturday 6 June was Westhoughton Homing Society Coronation Race, parties etc. There were also exhibitions in the library of paintings, Elizabethan style furniture, and documents from the first Elizabethan period from the County Record Office. The parade on Coronation Day was the biggest since the pre-war gala days of pre war. The programme was carried out in full, despite rain from 11.00 a.m. to 1.30 p.m.

Councillors and officials inspecting property in Manchester, May 1960, following the decision in 1958 to help in the housing of Manchester people. The men shown above include: Frank N. Walker (surveyor), Cllrs Adam-Glover, W. Raines, Fred Sharples, Harry Green, Reuben Greenhalgh, Hugh Booth, Mr Bibby, (treasurer), Fred Bolton, Fred Kelly, Dr Hollis Taylor (Ministry Of Housing), Wilson Astall (sanitary inspector). The overspill for Westhoughton was first mooted by Lancashire County Council in July 1951, with proposals to accommodate 20,600 people from Salford. A draft town map, providing for an estimated population of 41,100 by 1971, was drawn up in 1952, but with no decisions likely before 1960. Later Salford decided that overspill developments at Worsley and Irlam would meet their requirements. After Manchester City Council had twice been refused permission to develop at Lymm, the Minister of Housing suggested Westhoughton. Westhoughton UDC approved the proposal after the Lancashire County Council approved it. In 1960 Manchester wanted to try a pilot overspill scheme for 250 houses, but Westhoughton wanted a more comprehensive development, with industry to keep people within the district. Manchester agreed to develop along these New Town lines; a joint development committee was formed, and in 1962 a town map was submitted providing for the large scale development of the town, increasing the population from 17,000 to 71,000. The council's concern was to revitalise a town which had experienced declining employment, and they could see a time when there would be no collieries, even nearby. 'The project is a blueprint for youth and the new Westhoughton will be a thrilling place in which to live, work, and play. The project is a vast one, but will provide a town with every cultural and artistic amenity.' (photograph courtesy of *Horwich and Westhoughton Journal*)

August 1963. Anti-Overspill Association
Fighting Fund Office, Cllr A. Woods and
interested onlookers. There had been opposition
before, but when the map was put on public
display, Westhoughton people realised the full
implications of the proposal, and were concerned
to preserve their identity. Many people were
shocked to find that 1,500 of the 5,760 houses in
the town would have to be pulled down to make
way for the new developments. Anti-Overspill
candidates who fought the elections in May 1963,
were elected, and at a meeting on 15 August
1963 council support became council opposition.
Meetings were long and bitter, and following
a CPO covering more than 3,000 acres, which
proposed the demolition of the whole of Market
Street, excluding the Town Hall, the Anti-
Overspill Association was officially established
and the town was in uproar. The outcome of this
was the announcement of a public enquiry, to be
held at the Albert Hall, Bolton, as the Carnegie
Hall was thought to be too small for the large
number of objectors expected. (photograph
courtesy of *Horwich and Westhoughton Journal*)

Overspill protest march, October 1963, when the public enquiry opened at the Albert Hall. A
planning expert at the enquiry said, 'Westhoughton was a straggling, characterless, and dying town.'
People though were afraid of being absorbed and 75% of the electorate signed a petition against it.
After the enquiry, which was the longest on record at that time, the Housing Minister, Sir Keith
Joseph agreed to the proposals, but said that there should not be any wholesale demolition of existing
properties, although this excluded properties in the Hart Common and Marsh Brook districts.
However, there was no progress to implement the scheme, because of a difference of opinion about
the terms of reference for the consultants. As a result, the new Housing Minister, Sir Anthony
Greenwood, withdrew Government support for the scheme in October 1966, because of the conflict
between Westhoughton and Manchester. It had been a long and weary road and for most people there
was relief that the years of uncertainty, indecision and tension were at an end. (photograph courtesy
of *Horwich and Westhoughton Journal*)

Old Bridge, Hall Lee Bank Park. The park was opened in 1910, and was given to the town by Sir William Rothwell Hulton. The land was previously in a valley known as The Bank, and took its name from being part of the old Leigh Hall estate. Squire Hulton (William) purchased the estate in 1809. The Hall was a moated manor house, and Hall Lee Bank, and Lee Hall Bank are both names used on different maps. Coal was mined in the valley as early as 1764, and there are references to colliers belonging to Hall Lee Bank Colliery in 1831. The ornamental gates were installed in February 1938.

Westhoughton Market, 1952. In 1900 the market was open apart from some wooden booths for vendors of green grocery, fish and poultry. Regular stall holders were 'Owd Blatheraway' who sold books, and Prof. Allen who sold bottles that cured anything from baldness to bunions, Tape worms were displayed in bottles as 'orrible examples' of what one could get if the medicine was not taken daily. All the traders seemed to have the gift of tongues, especially Gypsy Sarah and her parakeet, who told fortunes for one piece of silver, or three coppers, 'just this once', if that is all you had. Lumbo Tigo extracted teeth using only his fingers, and sold the world famous Lumbo Tigo tooth cleaning powder, ground from the roots of bushes found only in the swamps of Georgia. Every few weeks some kind of 'show' would visit. These were often just a small shabby circus, smelly menagerie, or travelling theatre, but to visit them was really wonderful.

Two

War

Westhoughton's memorial to the men who were killed in the First World War was threefold. The council purchased and equipped a motor ambulance, bought Sunny Bank and furnished it as a clinic, and on the space among the trees in front of the building, erected a Cornish granite cross with the names of the fallen on the base. From a population of 15,000, 1,600 men went to fight. Of these, 201 were killed, 37 were taken prisoners of war, and 38 were awarded military decorations. There would have been more but for the number of young men killed in the Pretoria Pit disaster in 1910. Col. Crosfield, D.S.O., unveiled the memorial cross, on Saturday 28 July 1923, 'to the glory of God and to the inspiration of all people here in Westhoughton and to all who come afterwards.' 'Westhoughton may be proud of the part she played in the war,' the Colonel added. 'The roll of honour entailed great sorrow to mothers and wives who gave their menfolk, he knew, but he urged them to let this occasion rouse their pride because their men were noble.' After the ceremony an unending stream of people passed by the cross.

Peace Celebrations, 1919. This waggon was part of the carnival procession for the peace celebrations. It was provided by the Co-op., and Britannia was Mary Elizabeth Parr. The man holding the horse is James Baxter, a Wingates butcher. In front of the waggon, left to right are: -?- , Harry Clark, Jack Haughton, John Bullough, Walter Haughton, Thomas Smith Hibbert (butcher). (photograph courtesy of Mr W. Hibbert)

Certificate presented to Frank Smith

Peace celebrations, 30 November 1918. The end of the First World War, and the armistice signed two weeks earlier, were celebrated in Westhoughton with the public roasting of an ox. The ox, given by William Heaton of Lostock, a cattle dealer and mill owner, was slaughtered behind the Red Lion, and roasted on the historic mill site at the corner of Mill Street and Market Street. The spindle on which the beast was roasted was apparently specially made for the occasion at the old Gun Works, James Street. People came from miles around to see the spectacle and thousands of school children were given ox sandwiches and copies of a 'dainty card ' as a souvenir. (photograph courtesy of L. Basnett)

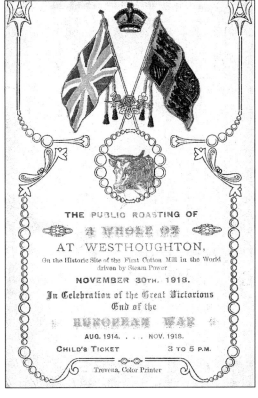

Peace celebrations, ox roasting ticket, 30 November 1918. Three thousand people tucked into the roast ox sandwiches. Some of the meat was a bit underdone, according to eyewitness Herbert Partington of Morris Green. The fires for the ox roasting were laid as early as 6 a.m. There is a brass plaque in the library commemorating the presentation of the head of the ox to the township of Westhoughton.

THE PUBLIC ROASTING OF
A WHOLE OX
AT WESTHOUGHTON,
On the Historic Site of the First Cotton Mill in the World driven by Steam Power

NOVEMBER 30TH. 1918.

In Celebration of the Great Victorious End of the

EUROPEAN WAR

AUG. 1914. . . . NOV. 1918.

CHILD'S TICKET   3 TO 5 P.M.

Trevena, Color Printer

The Town Hall, sandbagged. At the outbreak of the Second World War, Cllr Cowburn's message to local people was to be calm and courageous. He knew that Westhoughton people would 'display the courage that all colliery communities were renowned for'. There was a lot of activity in the first week, and on 8 September 1939, the full list of air raid wardens' posts was issued. These were at the rear of the Wheatsheaf Hotel; a house at the Grove, Wigan Road; the Colliery Institute, James Street (headquarters); rear of The Royal Oak, Fourgates; a house in Wigan Road, Hart Common; a house in Leigh Road, Daisy Hill; No. 272 Bolton Road, White Horse; Next to Stag and Griffin, Chequerbent; 114 Newbrook Road, Over Hulton and Near Model Laundry, St Helens Road. Each post was sandbagged and volunteers, mostly children, filled the first bags on the Red Lion field.

Air raid precautions, 1939. Twelve hundred Anderson shelters were erected and 250 wardens were appointed, 37 of whom were full-time. Fourteen ARP Wardens were on duty every night in Westhoughton. Mothers of children under 2 were summoned for a demonstration of anti-gas devices for babies and the blackout regulations were explained to the public.

Stirrup pump demonstration, July 1940. The method of extinguishing an incendiary was explained and demonstrated to the residents of Waters Nook.

An ARP stretcher party at work outside Westhoughton County Primary School, Central Drive. In the picture are: T. Hart, J. Byers, Tom Berry, W. Morris, J. Irwin, Wilfred Goastrey, Harry Green, Leonard Morris, Jim Morris, John Greenhalgh, Margaret Bradley, and A. Halliwell. (photograph courtesy of *Horwich and Westhoughton Journal*)

Lady Antrim, officially opening a hostel for war workers at Hilton House, the area near the Georgian House, on 25 April 1941. The war brought money and work to the cotton and mining industries. £579,638 went back to the Government in 4 savings weeks. (photograph courtesy of *Horwich and Westhoughton Journal*)

War Weapons Week parade, passing the Victoria Inn on Market Street. The week began on Saturday 17 May 1941, with military and civil parades taken by Sir James W. O'Dowda, at the Town Hall. The RAF, WAAF, ATS, Home Guard, Civil Defence, British Legion, WVS and Councillors, as well as a contingent of Polish airmen all took part. The original aim was to raise £60,000 in savings and investment. This was soon achieved and progress was recorded on an indicator outside the Town Hall, which was changed daily at 11.00 a.m. (photograph courtesy of *Horwich and Westhoughton Journal*)

The crowd watching the parade are outside the shop next to the Victoria Inn on Market Street. 'Double it' was the slogan and the final total raised was £150,000, enough to buy seven heavy bombers. This was a remarkable total for a depressed area. Westhoughton schools alone collected £10,000. Ten years old Joan Tinniswood of Market Street put every subscription she collected into a patchwork pocket on a pinafore, and then sent this, with the pockets sealed, to the clerk of the District Council, Mr B. Anson, who had the job of counting the money. Other events during the week were a Sunday concert at the Empire Cinema, displays by the Auxiliary Fire Service, films, and a display of war weapons in the Carnegie Hall. (photograph courtesy of *Horwich and Westhoughton Journal*)

Warship Week. Westhoughton ATC on a march past during Warship Week, which began on Saturday 21 March 1942. Cllr Berry, Lord Crawford, Cllr Howarth, and Commander Dickson are on the steps. The aim of the week, which was opened by the Earl of Crawford and Balcarres, was to raise £136,485 in savings to adopt the minesweeper *HMS Bridgewater*. He said that Aspull, Westhoughton, and London were having savings weeks. Aspull had had the temerity to challenge Westhoughton to raise more money, so why shouldn't Westhoughton challenge London. Beneath the thermometer recording progress, was a painting of *HMS Bridgewater*, done by employees of Wigglesworths. Westhoughton raised £140,924 and Aspull, £66,825; London's figure is not known. The library has a plaque on display commemorating the adoption of the minesweeper. (photograph courtesy of *Horwich and Westhoughton Journal*)

Some of the London evacuee children who arrived at the Wingates reception centre on Wednesday 12 July 1944. Cllr Sutcliffe, chairman of the council, is on the left. Ninety-five children aged between 5 and 14 were among the first contingent, spending the night in Wigan, then travelling by motor bus to Wingates Independent Methodist School, where a welcome had been prepared. They got out of the buses, most carrying small cases, but others had brown paper parcels with their contents falling out. Some clung to dolls and all had gas masks. A typical example of the evacuees was Irene from Islington, aged 9, with her two brothers, aged 11 and 5. The first job was to make sure they were all clean. Dr Leigh, the Medical Officer of Health, carried out a medical inspection, looking for skin trouble or dirty heads, followed by registration, with every child given a label on the lapel of their coat. After dinner the task of finding foster parents began and an urgent appeal for billets was made. Cllr Sutcliffe appealed for people to show sympathy and love and to take these children to their hearts. He said that they have come here to get restful sleep and to play without fear of the 'buzzing bombs' Free medical attention was promised and the WVS provided clothing and bedding, and beds too, if people had room but no beds. The billeting allowance was 10s 6d a week for under-fives, rising on a scale to 17s 6d for those aged 17 plus. All enquiries about billeting were dealt with at the library. A total of 294 London women and children came to Westhoughton to escape the flying bombs, staying at rest centres at the Parochial School, Trinity Methodist School, and Wingates before being billeted. Families were kept together, one woman and 8 children being billeted at the Technical School in Market Street, where adaptation included the erection of cubicles. Mr Taylor of Taylor and Hartley provided a wooden hut in the works yard, with a kitchen and other facilities, for a mother and her 5 children. This was a Mrs Biles who said, 'Westhoughton people are marvellously warm hearted' (photograph courtesy of *Horwich and Westhoughton Journal*)

Fourgates Victory Party 1945. The announcement of the end of the war at midnight on 15 August 1945 brought people onto the streets and into the town centre, surpassing even the VE Day celebrations. Within half an hour 2,000 people had gathered around the Market Street and Church Street corner. The church bells rang out, and Cllr Simkin, the chairman of the council, invited the crowd to join in the singing of 'there'll always be an England'. At 2 a.m., there was a silent tribute to those who had died, and at 3 a.m., there was a call for volunteers to accept the 'freedom of the microphone', to sing and entertain. Victory parties took place everywhere, one of the most impressive being at Dobb Brow, which had a miniature platform, complete with piano and loudspeakers to relay the highlights of all the BBC programmes. (photograph courtesy of *Horwich and Westhoughton Journal*)

Miss Ethel Hilton, of Church Street, represented the Bolton and District Card Room Workers in the Victory Parade. One of the best parties in the district was at the Wearish Lane housing estate, which had teas, sports, dancing, illuminations, a bonfire, a potato pie supper, and a crooning competition. Children of the George Street area had their own trial of war criminals, burning an effigy of Hitler at the stake, followed by a cricket match, games and competitions. Sunday 19 August was observed as a day of thanksgiving for peace. One thousand four hundred Westhoughton men and women had served in the Second World War, and the memorial to those who died on active service was unveiled and dedicated on Sunday, 7 November 1948. The cenotaph lists 109 men who died on active service. A memorial in the Town Hall was dedicated to their memories on November 1992.

Wellington Inn. The memorial was unveiled to the memory of twenty service members of the Wellington Inn Comforts Fund who were killed in action. Seven friends, headed by Licensee, Chris Waring, decided to start a comforts fund of their own for men and women of the district in the forces. They ran weekly competitions to raise cash and had a permanent sign written board with names on in the pub. Their efforts made the national press and at the end of the war a memorial was erected to those who gave their lives. The pub was later demolished, with last orders being in November 1970. The memorial was given to the library, where it is on display today. Westhoughton people were very concerned for the men and women in the forces. The British Legion, for instance, sent out 12,500 parcels, and was awarded the Haig Cup in 1943 for being the best branch in the country. (photograph courtesy of *Horwich and Westhoughton Journal*)

Don't panic! An unexploded bomb is discovered on land near Hilton House on 29 April 1946. Mr J. Scott of Park Hall Farm was working in one of his fields planting potatoes, when his horse shied. Mr Scott discovered a hole in the ground 12 inches in diameter, and five or six yards deep. From the size and shape it seems certain that at the bottom of the hole lay a German bomb. It was possibly dropped on 30 August 1940, when bombs were dropped in the vicinity, probably aimed at the Manchester to Preston railway line nearby.

Three

Work

'From mill and mine the signal ran – there's nowt like a Howfen man'

Westhoughton Old Factory. This was situated at the junction of Market Street and Bolton Road, on a site now used as a car park. This mill, built by Richard Lockett in 1803 was burned on 24 April 1812 by a mob of Luddite rioters – an event of national importance, which had a serious impact on the town's industrial prospects. The mill was one of the first to be steam powered, fifteen power looms having been transferred from Stalybridge by the owners Rowe and Dunscough and local people saw this factory system as a threat to their livelihoods. By 1811 the distress among handloom weavers, of which there were a large number in Westhoughton, was terrible, with low average earnings and a shortage of food. The expense of the war against Napoleon was crippling the economy, and people were starving. Militant workers, Luddites, took matters into their own hands, attacking factories in other manufacturing areas. Westhoughton Mill became the focus for a desperate protest, and was the most serious incident in Lancashire.

Factory Nook, opposite the mill site. A plaque on the wall, at the end of the row, commemorates the event. One of the men who encouraged the Luddites was an 'informer', John Stones, and he was part of a network of government spies, organized by local magistrate Ralph Fletcher. He acted as an agitator, recruiting and organizing men to attack the mill. On the 24 April, employees armed by the militia guarded the building, but they left when they heard that a mob was on its way from Chowbent (Atherton), arriving at 3 p.m. The mill manager went to Bolton for the militia, but by the time they arrived 170 looms and bales of cloth had been set alight.

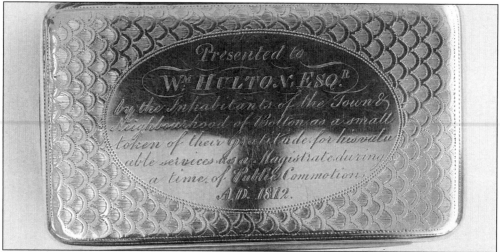

Snuffbox presented to William Hulton for his valuable services as a magistrate in 1812. After the burning, a number of suspects were arrested, based on the names given by Stones to Fletcher, though it was claimed that some had no connection with the incident. Fourteen prisoners were committed to Lancaster Gaol by Fletcher, acting with two local magistrates, the Revd William Hampson, and William Hulton of Hulton Park. Job Fletcher, 'Lame Jim' Smith, Thomas Kerfoot, and a crippled boy aged about thirteen, Abraham Charleston, whose only offence was to break a window with his crutch, were sentenced to death, and hanged. Six others charged with administering the Luddite oath were sentenced to seven years transportation. Thomas Holden, one of those transported, wrote to his family from Sydney, and copies of some of those letters are in the library. The snuffbox is now kept in the Bolton Museum. (photograph courtesy of Bolton Museum)

Westhoughton Old Factory, c. 1900. After the fire Rowe and Dunscough rebuilt their mill at Stalybridge, and other mill owners refused to invest in Westhoughton, resulting in a period of poverty and stagnation in the town for over thirty years. Rather than becoming a centre of the textile industry, it was considered in 1842 to be the poorest of the twenty-five townships comprising the Bolton Union. Later on the factory was used as a corn mill and again for textile manufacture. The chimney was struck by lightning several times and was rebuilt in 1856, on which occasion the Westhoughton Old Band played music from the upper platform. The mill fell into decay and was eventually demolished in 1900, the chimney following on 25 March 1901.

Manchester Road, Wingates around 1900, with the Albion Mill on the right. R.C. Haworth's mill employed 200 people, and contained 38,504 mule spindles, 4,228 ring spindles, and 3,276 doubling spindles. Mrs Clarke, of No. 40 Chorley Road, retired in 1928, having begun work at Haworth's as a half-timer when she was 9 years old. At that time the factory hours were from 6 a.m. to 6 p.m. during the week, and from 6 a.m. to 2 p.m. on Saturdays. When she achieved full-time status she brought home 7s 6d each week.

The mill on fire on Wednesday, 31 August 1938. The fire began at about 4 p.m. and the cause was thought to have been friction on one of the mules. The mill was evacuated and by 5.30 p.m. was a blazing inferno, although it was said that 'workers covered up their machinery before dashing for the door'. Occupants of houses immediately adjoining the mill had to remove their furniture and leave their houses for safety. The fire service, coming from Atherton, were delayed at the Reform Club on Park Road by Silcocks Wakes vehicles manoeuvring into position on the factory field. The fire was a disastrous blow for a town already suffering from the industrial depression. Older workers were in tears because of the difficulty they knew they would have in finding other jobs.

Weavers on strike at West Grove Manufacturing Company's Allenby Mill, 11 April 1945. Pictured from left to right are Mrs Marriner, Mrs Ryley, Alice Hibbert, and Mrs Pilkington – they are being paid for the small part of the week that they worked. One employee refused to join the union because she objected to the way contributions were paid and the other 150 workers refused to work alongside her. At the time of the strike 20,000 yards of cloth a day were coming off the looms. After a week the girl agreed to join the Weavers Association and work resumed on 12 April. The mill later became part of the Taylor and Hartley Group. (photograph courtesy of *Horwich and Westhoughton Journal*)

Allenby Mill, 5 November 1948. There were presentations to Miss E. Pennington of Hart Common on her retirement from the Allenby Mill after fifty-four years service in the cotton trade. Long service was a feature of mill life, loyalty and dedication being prevalent throughout the industry. This length of service was not uncommon, and the *Journal* includes several references to long service. In 1928, Mr Wallwork of No. 311 Church Street retired after fifty-nine years at the Victoria Mills, having started work as a half-timer at 1s 3d per week. (photograph courtesy of *Horwich and Westhoughton Journal*)

Clogmaking, February 1940. One of the area's leading clogmakers secured contracts for hundreds of pairs for the Women's Auxiliary Territorial Service and for munition workers. These clogs had rubbers instead of irons. In 1941 the Government restricted supplies of upper leather to shoe manufacturers. In 1932 there were nine cloggers in Westhoughton, as well as a service at the Westhoughton Co-op. However after 1961, you had to go out of Westhoughton to get your clogs repaired. The war years were good for cloggers and the clogger's shop is a special memory for most people. Bob Dobson writes, 'it was invariably ill lit, with the dust of years everywhere, and the aroma of real leather. On a wooden bench, customers would wait in their stockinged feet.' Read all about clogs in *Concerning Clogs* by Bob Dobson, Dalesman Books, 1979, and *Clattering Clogs*, by Bob Dobson, Landy Publishing, 1981.

John Taylor and Sons' ropeworks in Chequerbent just before closure in April 1971. The family firm, established in 1870 in premises in Lever Street, Bolton, as Ford and Taylor, became John Taylor and Sons in 1886. In its heyday the firm employed 100 people at three factories – Bolton, Chequerbent and Chorley. Its success was built up on the supply of ropes for driving mill machinery, including the heavy ropes which used to provide the transmission of power from the massive mill steam engines. They imported hemp from Italy, flax from Belgium, and jute from India, and among their other products were bacon twine, skip and bag twine for mills, bundling twine, stitching twine, and lorry ropes. These products were sent all over the world. The Chequerbent factory used the old twisting method of making the rope and twine on a rope-walk, which was just behind Chequerbent station. The firm, which had a work force of twenty-two, went out of business voluntarily. Tom Anderton, the works manager, and the foreman, Harry Hallam, had both worked for the firm for forty years. (photograph courtesy of *Horwich and Westhoughton Journal*)

Taylor and Hartley's Mill, Christmas 1948. Before the Second World War, Westhoughton could lay claim to 2 spinning mills at Wingates, and 5 weaving sheds – Allenby, Hall Lee, Perseverance, Industrial and Glebe. All five of these weaving sheds eventually became part of the Taylor and Hartley Group; two men, Taylor and Hartley, who came to Westhoughton from Burnley in 1911, founded the firm. The mill was the centre of peoples' lives, and a considerable number worked in the textile industry. In 1921, 60% of all working females living in Westhoughton, worked in the mills. By 1963 this had fallen to 22%. Taylor and Hartley employed 64 men and 277 women in 1963. (photograph courtesy of *Horwich and Westhoughton Journal*)

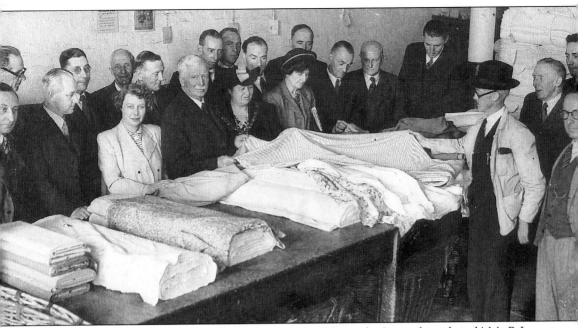

Taylor and Hartley's mill, August 1948. 'Britain's bread hangs by Lancashire thread.' Mr R.J. Davies, the town's MP, Cllr Mrs Kettle, chairman of Westhoughton Council, fellow councillors and officials paid a civic visit to several Westhoughton mills. Mr H. Haslam, mill manager, is showing samples of fabrics woven in Westhoughton at Taylor and Hartley's mills to members of the official party, who also include W. Shackleton, Revd Dimmock, Mr and Mrs Lyth (clerk to the UDC), T. West, T.H. Walker (surveyor), J. Blears, and J. Grundy. The main product was grey cloth and fine dress cottons. The firm also had making up concerns such as Fourgates Garments of Chorley Road. One reason behind this official visit was that at this time after the war, there was a need to restore the economy and the workers in the textile industry were urged to take a lead. Herbert Morrison, Lord President of the Council, in a speech at Manchester earlier in the same year said 'When I call upon the men and women of the cotton industry to take the lead in the fight for economic recovery I am calling upon them to strike a blow not only for prosperity but for peace. This is the nation's call to cotton. This is the cotton industry's finest hour.' (photograph courtesy of *Horwich and Westhoughton Journal*)

Taylor & Hartley

(Textile Holdings) Ltd.

Cotton & Spun Rayon Manufacturers

Westhoughton Carnival, c. 1920. The procession is at Diddy Bottle Park, Church Street, with John Chadwick's silk mill in the background. From 1826 silk weaving was introduced to Westhoughton as a cottage industry, and by 1841 silk weaving was the major occupation. In 1851, John Chadwick, inventor and silk manufacturer, built Peel Mill, as well as operating two other local mills, employing over 700 people. After the Luddite riots he was considered a 'bold man to build a mill in Westhoughton'. He was awarded an 'Honourable Mention' at the Paris Exhibition in 1855 for the taste and skill of the Westhoughton silk weavers. He also built Brookfield in 1851. In 1892 he sold the mill and the house to Thomas Dunkerley of Macclesfield. The mill was used by James Wigglesworth from 1915, and demolished in 1983 for housing.

'Sunny Bank', and the house adjoining, 'South View', were built in 1853. Mr Chadwick had eight daughters and four sons. One of his sons died aged twelve in 1862, and another was drowned at Fingal's Cave in August 1884. Under the trees is a fountain erected in memory of his two sons, presented to the Local Board in September 1885. This was later moved to the small park opposite the cenotaph. The Revd Peter Ditchfield, Westhoughton's greatest man of letters, and the 'historian of the English village', was born there. There is an almost complete collection of his works in Westhoughton Library.

Tablet filling at Wigglesworth's, Church Street, around 1960. In 1915, James Wigglesworth took over the mill for his pharmaceutical business, and played a prominent part in the life of the town for 50 years. He was born in Dewsbury and came to Bolton in 1895, to an appointment in a chemist's shop. He started business in Duke Street, Bolton in 1907, before transferring to Westhoughton. The business flourished and 6 years later he opened a branch in Dublin. The firm employed 250 people in the 1960s and 'the pill factory' made everything from indigestion tablets to hand cream and medicated sweets. The factory was completely self-contained, carrying out every process of manufacture and packing, including printing, box making, and design of labels. Jobs at the factory included tablet filling, putting colouring and sugar coating on unpleasant tasting tablets, and filling bottles with nasal solution, wart solvent, toothache tincture, and corn solvent. In 1960, 360 indigestion tablets were made each minute. (photograph courtesy of *Horwich and Westhoughton Journal*)

Wigglesworth's Employees at their Christmas Party, 7 January 1949. Mr Wigglesworth inspired great affection and devotion in his employees. At the time of the 1926 general strike he opened up the facilities of his works canteen to provide a soup kitchen, so that the children at least could be ensured of a good hot meal. Later, in the dark days of the depression in the 1930s he was President of the Unemployed Allotments Association. (photograph courtesy of *Horwich and Westhoughton Journal*)

 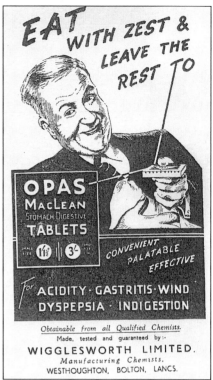

Left: James Wigglesworth being made a Freeman of Bolton, 13 December 1963. He was a great philanthropist who gave many gifts to Bolton, and this was recognised when he was made a Freeman of Bolton, the 11th in the history of the town. He contributed substantially to the improvement scheme in Victoria Square, paying for floodlit fountains, trees, additional seats, and areas of lawn around the war memorial, believing it was important for industrial towns like Bolton to be made as attractive as possible. Other gifts included a portrait of the Queen by Devas, which hangs in the mayor's parlour, a mayoral jewel for wear in place of the mayoral chain with evening dress, the £7,000 Chapel of Meditation at Overdale, the open air theatre and conservatory at Queens Park, and the improvement to the Chorley New Road frontage of the park. Mr Wigglesworth was a president and benefactor of Bolton Lads Club, a supporter of Bolton Little Theatre, and a founding member of the Bolton Rotary Club. He was connected with many other organizations and groups in the district, working tirelessly on their behalf until his death in March 1966, aged 90. He was one of Bolton's People of the Millennium, whose generous gifts were of benefit to us all. (photograph courtesy of *Horwich and Westhoughton Journal*)

Right: Advertisement for Wigglesworth's, 1953.

Rigby's Smithy, Queen Street, c. 1912. The firm was started by John Rigby, known as Smithy Jack, and continued by his two sons. Before the war the Rigbys had one hundred farmers on their books, with ten horses shod every day. Three men were permanently employed shoeing horses all day long. It closed in 1966, after sixty-three years, due to changes in farming methods. In that year it was said that they might not get more than one horse a week, but other jobs might include mending a loom at a mill, making a wrought iron gate, an urgent repair to a combined harvester, or a ring cutting from a swelled finger.

Mr Dick Pass, who with his brother owned Higher Barn Farm, Marshbrook, Westhoughton, was still doing his own ploughing on 20 April 1951, two months short of his seventy-fifth birthday. Farming, especially in Westhoughton, was a battle against the elements; in 1951 farmers were a month behind with ploughing, and Dick did not believe in tractors. Westhoughton relied on cotton and coal for employment but still always had the air of a market town, being surrounded by farms. As late as 1935 it was a home for eighty-two dairies and twelve slaughterhouses. (photograph courtesy of *Horwich and Westhoughton Journal*)

Vale Mill. The mill was built in the 1700s as a water-powered corn mill. The miller was Mr Haddock whose descendants, Alice Makant and Margaret Haddock, gave the money to build Daisy Hill Parish church. The building later became a bleach works and then a cotton waste factory. The millpond was stocked with fish until the closure of Eatock Pit which caused pollution; so in 1951 the pond was filled in. Harold Fairhurst, an archaeology enthusiast, dug up many relics of the old corn mill. He bought the mill and house in 1930, eight years after Albert Bannister's cotton waste concern went out of business. His enthusiasm for old mills was such that he bought another mill at Scorton near Lancaster. The mill building was listed as a building of historic interest until 1987, when the outlying townships of Bolton Metropolitan Borough were re-listed.

Charnley's pickle factory 1970. In 1938, the mill was used as a pickle factory by Charnley's Ltd. The business was founded in 1872, on a farm on Smithills Moor, near Horrocks Scout, later moving to premises in Bella Street, Daubhill, of which it was said in 1899 that 'there is no private home, in which more dainty care and cleanliness are observed than in the pickle factory of Mr Charnley.' Onions were imported from Egypt, and cauliflowers from the continent, but the vinegar was British. (photograph courtesy of *Horwich and Westhoughton Journal*)

Four

Mining

Pitheads next to wheatfields.

Miners were the 'knights of the pick and pitlamp' but they had to provide their own tools, and pay to have their picks sharpened, and they needed this done every day. These men are pick sharpeners, and are at Scot Lane Pit, Blackrod. Working conditions were harsh and primitive, and the accident rate and loss of life was shocking. The human price of coal was high. In the 1930s a Bolton dentist complained about some Trencherbone cobbles being half a crown a bag. The coalman said to him quietly, 'a miner has gone down into the bowels of the earth to get that coal for thee. It's the best coal that can be bought. It's been brought up on the shaft, screened, and sent in a wagon to the sidings. We've filled it, brought it out here, an' put a full hundredweight into thy coalshed for half a crown. If you think that's too much I'll bring it out again. Last week you charged my daughter six-and-sixpence to have a tooth out and it took you less than fifteen minutes. I don't see what you have to grumble about.' *Britain Revisited*, Tom Harrison. Gollancz. 1961.

Advertisement for picks.

Hewlett Pit, strike duty, 1912. The biggest strike Britain had ever witnessed began on 26 February 1912, with a million men out, in the fight for a minimum wage. Previously men working in abnormal places, where it was difficult to produce coal, had to depend on the under-manager to make their wages up to a reasonable amount. There was violence at the strike and the police called for military assistance. On 29 March, the Government passed the Coal Mines (Minimum Wage) Act, guaranteeing a minimum wage, and the men went back to work on 15 April. After 1870 there had been a dispute at the pit, when following the Franco-Prussian War Mr Hewlett called for a drastic reduction in wages, and a strike ensued. Newcomers came to work in the pits from Cornwall and the Forest of Dean, 'arriving at Crow Nest siding under a tar sheet'. For many years the remark, 'Thi fayther cum under th' tar sheet' was enough to start a fight at Dobb Brow or Hart Common. Alfred Hewlett was the son of the vicar of Astley, and one of the great mining engineers. He was managing director of the Wigan Coal and Iron Company. (photograph courtesy of Mr Forshaw)

EATOCK PIT, DAISY HILL in the 1920s

Owned by Wigan Coal & Iron Co.

Copied from Caleb Pamely's Colliery Manager's Handbook

Eatock No. 2 Pit, Daisy Hill, in the 1920s. The pit, near Hosker's Nook and Miry Lane was owned by the Wigan Coal and Iron Co. founded in 1865. The chairman in 1928 was The Rt. Hon. The Earl of Crawford and Balcarres of Haigh Hall, and the pit employed 313 men in that year. A feature of the company's collieries was that all the surface arrangements; sidings, workshops, etc. were very neat in appearance, and well laid out. The pit closed in 1936. The company also owned Hewlett's 1 and 2 pits in the town. Read more in *Wigan Coal and Iron* by Donald Anderson and A.A. France, Smiths Books, 1994.

Brancker Street, Chequerbent 1961. On the right are the slagheaps of Chequerbent pits, which closed in 1927. These houses were built by the Hulton Colliery Company for their employees, consisting of two, and three bedroomed properties, the largest houses being for senior employees. At the back, they were blocked by the private railway line linking the colliery with the main line, which ran in a cutting almost underneath their front doors. The street got its name because two Liverpool men, Richard and John Brancker were early directors of the company, Richard being listed as chairman and managing director in 1928. The street knew tragedy in abundance. After the Pretoria Pit explosion on 21 December 1910 there was hardly a house in the street that didn't have a coffin. A fourteen year old girl, Annie Lynch, who lived at No. 131, was a screen hand at the Pretoria Pit. She was killed when her skirt caught in a machine in April 1922. Demolition of the first block began in 1970 and was completed in 1974 when everyone had been found alternative accommodation. (photograph courtesy of *Horwich and Westhoughton Journal*)

Stotts Pit site in Church Street, 1972. It was owned by the Westhoughton Coal and Cannel Company. The house in the colliery yard, was the home of the under-manager. Cannel, or kennel, burns with a bright flame and is famous for the production of gas. It is similar to jet in many ways and can be carved into ornaments. The pit closed due to flooding. It was said that the trouble was due to water accumulated since the Aspull pumping pit closed down and that £5,000 spent then would have saved both Scot Lane and Stotts Pit. There had been controversy about this reluctance to spend the necessary money, and the use of 'industrial espionage', to monitor the situation. In March 1934 it was revealed that there was a huge lake of water underground at Scot Lane which might break through into a section of Stotts Pit at any time. The men were called out and this part was closed.

Stotts Pit flooding. Water broke into Stotts Pit on 14 November 1936 causing severe flooding. There was a fight to save the pit and the jobs of 500 people. Tons of cement were rushed to the scene of the flooding and a giant pump installed but this was to no avail, as 500 gallons a minute poured in. T. Bamber and T. Berry are emptying a tub of water on the surface in a battle to save the pit. The Westhoughton Coal and Cannel Company later claimed damages against the Wigan Coal Corporation for the flooding, but were unsuccessful. (photograph coutesy of Mrs A. Horrocks)

Men on the surface at Stotts Pit after the flooding. Stotts pit was Westhougton's last pit in a district that was once considered one of the high spots in the Lancashire coalfield. In 1921, 55% of all resident occupied males in the town were mineworkers. When the pit closed in 1936 it resulted in the worst figures for unemployment in Westhoughton for a long time, with 1,231 men unemployed. Although reserves of coal still existed, mainly at great depth, the cost of reopening the waterlogged workings was considered prohibitive, even during the post-war period of coal shortages. In 1934 'back to the land' was the principal suggestion offered to Westhoughton people affected by the slump in the industrial situation, but there were no real alternatives. The chairman of the council, Cllr T. Sherrington, summed up the council's position, when he said that 'they had been brought in when the patient was nearly dead', and blamed the mine-owners for their lack of foresight. (photograph courtesy of *Horwich and Westhoughton Journal*)

A view of the pit showing the famous 'dump', or 'ruck' in the background, where the agent and manager, Mr H.O. Dixon, and his board of directors, allowed coal picking in hard times. In the 'dirt' that is sent up from the pits there is a certain amount of broken coal, and this could be picked out of the slag heaps. The depression bit deep, and men, women and children, came from far and wide.

Coal picking at Stott's Pit, February 1936. At the top of the heap, ragged looking men, each with a sack, and coal-hammer strapped under his coat tails, wait for the tubs of waste. As the tubs arrive at the top of the dump there is a rush as men scramble forward, despite the danger. Tuesdays and Thursdays are the most popular days, being days that the men do not have to sign on. Down below, women and children scrabble with their hands in the damp dirt to pick out small lumps of coal. All day long, over this grey mountain, people would be prising out the coal, among the sulphurous smoke and fumes. Due to internal combustion, the slag heaps were on fire under the surface. Sometimes there were as many as 200 pickers on the heap together, and this also happened at night when the pit was working a double shift. This constant picking and burrowing eventually gave the heap a hummocky appearance. Coal was taken away on home made trucks, or on bicycles, sometimes made from rusty parts found on refuse tips, the bags slung across the frame of the machine. The company's brickworks made 100,000 bricks a week from material taken from the heap but every day it grew in size. There wasn't another pit for miles around where this was allowed. It still went on elsewhere, but the colliery companies did sometimes prosecute. George Orwell describes the penury and misery of the people in *The Road to Wigan Pier*, Secker and Warburg, 1937. He outlines the techniques of survival to which men and women resorted; 'the scene stays in my mind as one of my pictures of Lancashire: the dumpy, shawled women, with their sacking aprons and their heavy black clogs, kneeling in the cindery mud and the bitter wind, searching eagerly for tiny chips of coal. They are glad enough to do it. In winter they are desperate for fuel; it is more important than food.' (photograph courtesy of *Bolton Evening News*)

A result of the depression was the opening of the Unemployed Social Centre for men on 26 July 1933, in a building at the old Westhoughton Gun Works, James Street. There had been a Royal Navy munitions factory on the site during the First World War, with cranes for lifting and moving great guns, but these were dismantled in 1925. The building was placed at the disposal of the unemployed by Mr H.O. Dixon, general manager of the Westhoughton Coal and Cannel Company and was adjacent to the Westhoughton Institute for Mineworkers, which had reading rooms, billiard rooms and other facilities. Members paid one penny a week subscription and an appeal for funds and equipment was made. Sewing machines, cooking utensils, chairs, games, books, magazines, tools and sports kit were among the items required. The men had a boot repairing bench, repairing thirty pairs of boots and twenty pairs of clogs in the first month.

The men also made Christmas toys for their own children. Mr J. Hargreaves, a member of the committee gave lectures, 'on letter writing' and 'applying for a situation' and the problems of the unemployed were discussed in debates. A wireless set was obtained from the BBC free of charge. A concert was held at the Empire Cinema to raise funds, entertainment being provided by the Horwich RMI Band and three vocalists. Similar facilities for women were provided at the Church Street Methodist School and both centres opened on the same day. Mothers were able to bring their young children along and take part in activities such as mothercraft, 'make and mend', and country dancing. The following year the scheme lost its headquarters at the Gun Works and the name was changed to the Westhoughton Unemployed Allotment Association, with all efforts being concentrated on inducing the unemployed to take up allotments.

Mr J. Gregory on his allotment in August 1936, preparing for the first show of members of Westhoughton Unemployed Allotments Association. The gardens adjoined the burning tip of the Starkie Pit, which closed in 1933. A large proportion of the unemployed men were miners and most had seen the headstocks of the pits where they worked dismantled, with few having any chance of getting back to the type of work for which they were trained. The show was held in the Carnegie Hall and only 22 men from 200 members entered. Many had little or no experience, and were nervous about competing with each other, but the entries were of a very high standard. The gold medal was won by Mr T. Shields, whose allotment won the most points. The proceeds from the show were donated to the local sick nursing association. The scheme had its origins in 1931 when local councils were encouraged by the Ministry of Agriculture to provide allotments for unemployed men. The purpose was 'to enable the unemployed, partially unemployed and seriously impoverished men and women to obtain and cultivate their allotment gardens, thus helping them to provide the best and most wholesome foodstuffs for their homes, occupation for the body, interest for the mind and to prove that they are willing and able to do good service for the community.' By 1935 there were four sites, at James Street, Mill Lane, Daisy Hill, Church Walks, and Top o' th' Slack. (photograph courtesy of *Horwich and Westhoughton Journal*)

WESTHOUGHTON UNEMPLOYED ALLOTMENTS ASSOCIATION

Hon. Secretaries:

E. PETERS. 4, Church Walks.   M. EDDISON. 24, Oxlea Grove.

Dobb Brow. The most ambitious scheme was at Oldfield Farm, Dobb Brow. In 1936, an eight-acre site was handed over to thirty-two men, each of whom was given a quarter of an acre of land and a poultry house, plus twenty-five head of poultry. The Society of Friends (Quakers) provided generous financial assistance enabling seed and equipment to be provided at half price; one two-stone bag of concentrated fertiliser was 2s, a spade blade with T-handle was 2s 3d, a fork with four prongs was 2s, cookery booklet 1d, hut construction booklet 3d, garden booklet written for the scheme 1d, and a standard collection of seventeen packets of vegetable seeds 1s 6d. (photograph courtesy of *Horwich and Westhoughton Journal*)

Dobb Brow, 1935. One member of the scheme, Mr Baldwin, an unemployed miner, went to Cambridge, where they didn't know what unemployment meant, to address a meeting in connection with the university town's effort to help the unemployed. He gave a graphic survey of the lives of the unemployed and the distress and suffering in the district, caused by the closure of so many pits.

'Peace, perfect peace, on this sceptered isle and happy breed of men, where mother is queen of every home, a blessed spot, this paradise, Dobb Brow.' Edmund Hibbert

Rhys Davies was the MP for Westhoughton from 1924 until 1951. He was born in Llangennach, in Carmarthen, working on a farm and then as a miner in the Rhonnda valley for ten years. He worked in the cooperative movement and as a trade unionist, and was on Manchester City Council. He was the ideal person to represent Westhoughton during these grim years. The percentage of unemployment for males in Westhoughton varied from 45.4% in 1930, to 55%, in 1932, and rose to 46% in 1936. When the pits closed due to flooding, and mills went on short time, business slumped. At the turn of the century there were thirty pits, but by 1936 there was only one. The last twelve pits which used to employ several thousand men, closed between 1929 and 1936. Three hundred and twenty-one children per day had free school meals in 1935. A clog fund was in existence for some years from monies collected voluntarily. Some children could not have gone to school but for this. The situation was as bad as anywhere in the country, as bad as Jarrow and 'special areas' such as Durham and Glamorgan, which received assistance from public funds. Rhys Davies made representations in the House of Commons for special status for the four coalmining townships of Westhoughton, Aspull, Blackrod and Hindley. He campaigned relentlessly for the unemployed, endeavouring to improve conditions. Few MPs have held one constituency for over twenty-five years. He was a pacifist, and from 1939-1945 stood alone in the House of Commons, but he never lost his ideals. He was 'a man of the people who never forgot the people', always 'striving to protect the bottom dog'. He died on 30 September 1954.

Westhoughton Poultry Society, *c.* 1930. Fifth from left, is Mr W. Hall, and second from right, Mr E. Cleary. Poultry keeping was part of the agricultural life of the town, and was a hobby for miner and millworker, with a regular column in the weekly paper, entitled 'in my garden and poultry pen'. It was a hobby born of necessity in the depressed 1930s. In 1934, J.B. Priestley said that, 'between Bolton and Preston you leave the trams, and fried fish shops and dingy pubs. The feature of this route, once you were outside the larger towns, seemed to me to be what we call in the North the 'hen runs'. There were miles of them. The whole of Lancashire appeared to be keeping poultry. Domestic fowls have always had a fascination for the North-country mill hands. The hen herself, I suspect, made a deep sub-conscious appeal to these men newly let loose from the roaring machinery. At the sound of her innocent squawking, the buried countryman in them began to stir and waken. By way of poultry he returned to the land, though the land he had may have been only a few square yards of cindery waste ground. Now, of course, sheer necessity plays its part too. We were going through the country of the dole.' From *English Journey* by J.B. Priestley, Heinemann, 1934. (photograph courtesy of *Horwich and Westhoughton Journal*)

Some things did not change, and coal picking still took place. After the war, coal was in short supply and it was the practice to eke out meagre coal supplies from pickings from the waste heap of the old Hewlett Pit, Hart Common. On 5 July 1946, John Hope, of Hart Street, decided to spend an hour on his return from work, picking coal, helped by ten children who gathered to sort the coal from the dirt he dug. Suddenly, the earth caved in and he was buried along with two children, David Gaffney (aged five) and James Silcock (aged eleven). Help was summoned and the three were rescued. Mrs Gaffney said that her coalman had not been for a month and that she had no coal apart from the pickings from the heap. The two boys, together with Mr Hope and relatives are pictured at the spot where they were buried. Humane bravery certificates were later issued to the rescuers. From left to right: Mrs Silcock, Mrs Hope, Mrs Mann, Mrs Gaffney, Madaleine Seton, James Silcock, Daniel Gaffney, Sandy Mann, Mr Hope. (photograph courtesy of *Horwich and Westhoughton Journal*)

Hewlett Pit, *c.* 1972. Remains of No. 1 shaft and the steam engine winding remains viewed from the South West. (photograph courtesy of Alan Davies)

Mining Recruitment in Bolton Road, 15 October 1946. After the war there was a need to recruit miners and a mobile cinema visited the town as part of a nation wide recruitment campaign. Many men already travelled outside Westhoughton to work in the remaining mines. The purpose was to re-educate the public, showing films of modern coal mining methods and publicising the government's plans for nationalisation, for improving conditions, and making the industry more efficient. The Ministry of Fuel and Power planned that from January 1947 every collier would receive a training course. 'Coal mining was at the beginning of great change, and with bare coalsheds, there was a need for black diamonds.' (photograph courtesy of *Horwich and Westhoughton Journal*)

T' Miner by Eric Holt

Ah'm sick o' workin' deauwn yon mine,
Ah'd rayther be weer t' weather's fine.
Weer t' swallers fly, an' t' winds are free,
Nay, t' pits ne'er bin a place fer me.

Fer years Ah've worked i' dust an' muck,
Wi t' roof propped up Ah scrawp an' duck.
Sum times Ah've ne'er sin t' sun aw wik!
Ah'm teyred o' clugs, an' spade, an' pick.

At t' mornings droppin' deawn i' t' cage,
Ah think Ah'd earn a betther wage
Shovin' nowt 'eyvier than a pen.
Ay my! Ah weeshed mi 'onds were clen.

Yet monny a frozzen winter's neet
Ah sit bi t' feyre, an' toast mi feet,
An' think eaw chilly life would be
Wi'eawt a feyre, an' chaps like me!

Eric Holt lives in Westhoughton and is president of the Lancashire Authors Association, an organization founded in 1909, to keep alive the traditions and interests of Lancashire dialect and history. New members are always welcome. He has won many prizes for his work, and over the border, in Farnworth, has the distinction of having a poem incorporated into a mural in the entrance to Farnworth Pool.

Five

The Pretoria Pit Disaster

'*Between Christmas Day 1910, and New Years Day, 1911, the different cemeteries presented appalling sights which no one will ever forget: the hearses, the mourning coaches, the long funeral processions, the throngs of bereaved widows and orphans, relatives and friends, the hundreds of visitors, all of them making their way to the last cold resting places. To see the people in tears, to hear the sobbing and sighing of the wives and children, brothers and sisters, was something beyond human endurance.*'

Revd A.L. Coelenbier, Rector, Sacred Heart Parish, Westhoughton, 1 January 1911

Memorial to the disaster in Westhoughton churchyard. The term men and boys is seen on all colliery accident memorials, boys playing a very important part as haulage hands and pony drivers etc. Seventy-eight boys died, all of them under 20 and many under the age of 17. Another 139 of the men were between twenty and thirty years of age, making a total of 217 deaths under the age of 30. One hundred and ninety-one were single men. (photograph courtesy of Alan Davies)

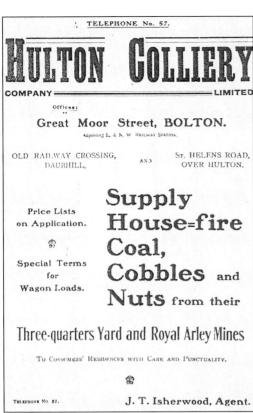

Lancashire's worst pit disaster and Britain's third largest loss of life from a single mining accident happened at the No. 3 Bank Pit belonging to the Hulton Colliery Company. The pit, known as the Pretoria Pit, was situated on Hulton Park land, on the border of Atherton and Westhoughton. It was considered then to be one of the safest and most modern in the British coal industry, having only been open to full production since 1903. Prior to the accident, the colliery raised 2,400 tons of coal per day, and employed 2,400 people. The Company had offices at Great Moor Street, adjoining the station, and depots at the Old Railway Crossing, Daubhill, and St Helens Road, Over Hulton. Deliveries were made to consumers' residences 'with care and punctuality.'

Pretoria Pit before closure in 1934. The explosion, about 300 yards below the surface, occurred at 7.50 a.m. on Wednesday, 21 December 1910. An eye witness said that 'it caused smoke and fumes to belch like a living volcano out of the two shafts, flinging timber and debris into the air, some to land on the adjoining winding house, followed by a huge cloud of dust which settled over the surrounding area. The ground around the pithead vibrated and the dull, heavy roar was heard up to four miles away. The full day shift had just begun and 898 men and boys were working below ground at that time. News spread quickly and hundreds of men, women, and children ran as fast as they could to the pit.

The scene at the pit. In the foreground is the Arley Pit, from which search parties started, and in the background is the Pretoria Mine. The General Manager, Mr Alfred Tonge who lived two miles away, heard the explosion, and arrived at the pit at 8.20 a.m. along with Dr Hatton, the surgeon to the colliery, and Sir William Hulton, on whose land the pits were situated. The first task was to repair damage caused to the gearing of the downcast, No. 4 shaft, in order to free the cage. Fortunately, the winding engine and apparatus were unaffected, and repairs were completed by 9.00 a.m. Mr Tonge, together with James Polley (electrical foreman), shaftmens – James Moss and John Hilton, and firemen – William Markland, John Hardman, Robert Roberts, John Herring and James Hartley, entered the pit, at great risk to themselves, as they were entering unknown and very dangerous conditions, with every risk of further explosions. They descended without breathing apparatus, but with safety lamps and caged canaries and mice to test for after damp. They received the King Edward Medal- the miners' VC.

Postcard showing the only survivors, sold to raise money for the victims' families. They rescuers proceeded down to the Yard level, where the explosion had occurred, but conditions there were too hazardous to investigate. One man, Fountain Byers, was found alive and the men returned to the surface with him but he died some days later in hospital. On the second descent Joe Staveley a young boy from the workshops was found alive, and together with William Davenport they were the only two survivors of all those working on the level where the explosion occurred. John Sharples, also rescued did not in fact survive, although he had recovered so well in the evening that he was on the point of being sent home from Bolton Infirmary, when he developed pneumonia, and later died.

Rescuers entering the pit. William Turton, a fireman, whose 2 sons were entombed in the Yard mine was overcome by fumes in trying to extinguish a fire, and he became the only rescuer to lose his life. On the first day 5 dead bodies were retrieved, among them the under-manager, Mr Edwin Rushton. They were taken to the joiner's shop, which for many weeks to follow was to be used as a temporary mortuary. The first team of trained rescuers on the scene was from the Howe Bridge Rescue Station. Sgt Major Hill, having heard of the disaster by telephone, arrived with his men, at 8.40 a.m. Others followed until there were 148 trained men at the mine, from Burnley, Accrington, Rishton, St Helens, Leigh, Bickershaw and elsewhere. During the day all 553 miners from the Arley and Trencherbone levels were gradually brought to the surface to be reunited with their anxious families. Various government officials arrived during the day, including Mr Gerrard, HM Inspector of mines for the district, and Mr R.A.S. Redmayne, the Chief Inspector of Mines.

By the close of day, there was considered little hope for the 336 men and boys still trapped. Hundreds of people gathered on the pit bank, forming an enormous and pitiful crowd, together with police, church leaders, surface staff, reporters, medical staff and the curious. They prayed, sang and listened to Dean Wellington of Manchester, Father Allen of Atherton and a Captain of the Salvation Army. Many stayed all night at the pithead, and dawn the next day revealed the full horror. Two lorries had earlier arrived with coffins for the dead. In the afternoon Mr Gerrard gave out an official statement. 'There is no hope, absolutely none, not the slightest shadow of hope at all of anybody being alive.'

The task of recovering the bodies began. In one day 123 bodies were brought up and after five days 270 bodies had been recovered. Most were hardly disturbed, deaths being due to carbon monoxide poisoning, but others were badly mutilated. Each body was numbered, and the exact whereabouts and conditions surrounding it were noted. The labelled corpses were brought to the surface and carried by the Saint Johns Ambulance men and other volunteers to the joiner's shop. Inside they were taken from wrappings, stripped, washed and placed in coffins.

Rescue workers and helpers at the scene. The man in the bowler hat is possibly a winding engineman and the be-medalled man, a rescue miner. On the right are pit brow workers. The engine house was prepared as an emergency station, while the Miners Union room was used as a temporary hospital. The Westhoughton district nurses, Nurses Gallimore, Jones and Green worked continuously, and Sarah Morgan, a pit brow worker, was on the scene for fifty hours attending to the welfare of the colliers and looking after the dead. On top of the coffins were placed any articles that might help identify their owners – tea cans, belts, clogs, scarves, stockings, and even a solitary apple. Among the belongings was a watch, stopped at 7.50 a.m., which is on display in Westhoughton Library. PC Green, among the contingent of police sent to the pit, identified one boy as his son. The body had been badly mutilated so he identified him by the belt he was wearing – he was just thirteen.

Westhoughton Council contributed a large vault for the unidentified bodies. Thirteen interments took place at a service conducted by the Revd Garrett, and among those laid to rest were the bodies of 4 boys aged about 14 years old. The final total of bodies unidentified at the time of burial was 24. The *Bolton Evening News* and *The Chronicle* published detailed descriptions wherever possible, of those unidentified. For example, 'Body No. 250. Tally No. 1159. Male aged about 26, round features, 5' 9", good teeth in upper jaw, none in lower jaw. Pair of clogs, 3 lace holes, size 9s, with leather laces, square toed, steel toecaps and newly ironed. Thin rope, apparently used as a belt, heather-mixture woollen ribbed stockings, far worn, light calico pit drawers, no buttons.'

From left to right, Samuel Pope (inquest barrister) John Gerrard (inspector of mines for the district) and Robert Nelson (electrical inspector of mines). On 23 December, the first inquests were held in the engine house, and the first complaints about the dangers of gas in the pit were made. On Christmas Eve, the first funeral took place, that of William Turton of Chequerbent. Thousands lined the streets on Christmas Day, to watch the funerals of seven victims, including that of Fountain Byers. On Boxing Day, 43 funerals took place, and there was scarcely a home in Wingates and Chequerbent without drawn blinds. On New Years Eve there were burials from dawn to dusk. A couple due to be married at Christmas, had to have the Church service at 5 a.m. to avoid meeting any funerals. By the 31 December, 290 bodies had been recovered but it took 9 more weeks for the remaining bodies to be recovered. By that time, 9 March 1911, the mine was again partly operational. Inquests later moved to the Carnegie Hall, where the main business was conducted. A jury of 18, including many mining experts, concluded that 'there was an accidental ignition of gas and coal dust on the conveyor face in the North Plodder mine, in some manner to the jury unknown, but probably from a defective or over heated safety lamp, and this produced an explosion.' The Home Office Enquiry, presided over by Mr R.A.S. Redmayne, HM Chief Inspector of Mines, opened on 20 February 1911 and lasted 18 days – 41 more witnesses were called. It was stated that the presence of coal dust extended the explosion, from the immediate area of the North Plodder to the rest of the mine. The major consequence of the enquiry was the passing of the 1911 Coal Mines Regulation Act, which repealed many previous acts, and included many of the recommendations of the enquiry, improving the standard of safety in Britain's coal mines. The bravery of the rescuers was noted in the official report and medals were awarded. Bolton Museum has 4 medals awarded to James Hartley, a fireman. These are the Edward Medal, 2nd class mines bronze medal, the St John of Jerusalem Life-saving Medal, the Royal Humane Society Medal, bronze, and the Bolton and District Humane Society Medal, bronze.

Ten men in a row of cottages at Waters Nook perished in the disaster. The enquiry and its aftermath were no consolation for a town that had suffered greatly. Of the 344 victims, 72 were from Bolton, mostly Daubhill, 23 from Atherton, and the rest were from Westhoughton and its districts, including 33 from Chequerbent, 23 from Daisy Hill, and 22 from Wingates. There was hardly a single household, which did not lose one of its members. William Cowburn, secretary of Wingates Band, left a wife and eleven children; Thomas Farrimond, a wife and eight children. These men were all active in the life of the town, in the church, drama societies, brass bands, cricket and football. Sacred Heart Football Club lost 12 of its 15 members; the Wingates Band lost its renowned soprano player, Albert Lonsdale, as well as four others members and its secretary. Chequerbent Harriers Athletic Club lost most of its members. National interest focussed on the town and two days afterwards the Mayors of Bolton, Manchester and Liverpool set up nation wide appeal funds. They generated a huge philanthropic response, raising £138,000 before being closed on 7 January 1911. Large donations included £2,000 from Australia, and £5,000 from the Liverpool Cotton Association. Many towns donated, and numerous different groups, including Surrey Farm Labourers. Football matches took place in Bolton and Barnsley, and the *Bolton Evening News* opened a fund, asking readers to send a shilling or more. At the pit head souvenirs were sold, including post cards and serviettes, and in the lane leading to the pit, a stuffed lion, with a collecting bag in its mouth, drew money from the morbidly fascinated visitors who spent Boxing Day there.

The memorial to the men in the Westhoughton Parish churchyard was unveiled on 25 November 1911. A widow received 4s, and 2s for each child, each week, from the Lancashire and Cheshire Miners Relief Fund, as well as similar amounts from the Trust Fund and compensation money from the Hulton Colliery Company. The Trust also gave £1,050 to the 88 victims of the explosion at the Cadeby Pit, Conisborough, on 9 July 1912 and the same amount to the 439 victims of the explosion at the Universal Colliery, Senghenydd, Glamorgan, on 14 October 1913 – Britain's worst disaster. There were five hundred and ninety-three beneficiaries who eventually received financial help from the Fund, which was wound up in 1975, when the last beneficiary died. The balance of £16,000 was handed over to the north-west area of the National Union of Mineworkers to support the Blackpool convalescent home.

A memorial plaque on the site of the disaster, at Broadway, off Newbrook Road, was unveiled on 19 September 1976, by Mr S.G. Vincent, General Secretary of the North Western Area of the National Union of Mineworkers. There are other memorials, including one on the wall of the Town Hall building, to those members of affiliated cricket clubs in the Bolton Cricket Association. In the library is a memorial from the Independent Order of Oddfellows Loyal Brothers Friend Lodge No. 1160, to twenty-one brothers of the lodge. Wingates Independent Methodist church has a memorial to those who lost their lives, and in the pulpit is a bible presented by the wife of Fountain Byers. He was the assistant choir master at Wingates Independent Methodist church. He had fifty boys working under him in the mine, with all of whom he was very popular. Poor lads, their fate was the most dreadful of all for they were in the main course of the explosion's blast.

Miners outside the Pretoria Pit on the day of closure, 14 April 1934. There were 750 miners employed before the closure, 400 of them from Westhoughton. They joined the 34% who were already unemployed in the town. It was said that amongst them was Joe Staveley, 1 of the 2 survivors of the disaster, as well as sons of many of those killed. The shafts were finally sealed on 21 December 1934, 24 years to the day of the explosion, which caused so much suffering.

Westhoughton Library has a large collection of material of all types about the disaster, including official reports, personal correspondence, poetry, theses, press cuttings, photographs and artefacts, and a comprehensive bibliography is available.

'Sleep, comrades sleep, give no thought to weary tomorrow,
Sleep on my lads, rest undisturbed, for the moment, forget your sorrow
Sleep comrades sleep, and dream of those you have left at home'

Words of a song to have been sung by Fountain Byers, at a concert on the evening of 21 December.

Six

Leisure

'Keep Folk Smiling' – The Houghton Weavers

Empire Cinema, Market Street, 1960. The Empire Cinema was opened on Empire Day, 24 May 1915, and was built for the Westhoughton Entertainment Company. The first manager, Jack Watkinson, was killed in the First World War. Later on Ted Clegg became the manager, Mrs Clegg was on the cash desk, and son Stanley was the chief operator. Two rows of seats used to be allocated each week to children from the Lostock Industrial School. In August 1930 the first 'talkies' with synchronised sound on disc were introduced. The equipment was described as the finest 'talkie' apparatus in the world, the British Thomson Houston Reproducer, and the first 'talkie' was The Desert Song. These didn't always operate smoothly because the cinema was located near a loop on the old tram track, and each time a tram crossed the points there was a grave danger of the needle jumping. However, the operators became adept at lifting the needle when a tram hit the points.

The cinema closed in November 1960, after falling attendances, and the cost of vandalism. In 1958, 100 seats had to be replaced because of malicious damage. The Empire was turned into a licensed social club, called the Casino Club. This was damaged by fire in 1963, and later was also known as the Gaiety. It was last used as a snooker club. (photograph courtesy of the *Bolton Evening News*)

The Empire Cinema held a special gift week, from 11-18 April 1940, for Westhoughton men and women serving in the armed forces. This was one of several schemes that the manager, Mr Gordon Clayton, (centre), introduced. At the presentation to launch the week, Miss Daisy Worthington is handing a parcel to driver J. Settle, of Church Lane, serving in the RASC. Mr Clayton went into the forces soon afterwards, and Miss Doris Ashton took over as manageress, having started work at the cinema in 1929 as a cashier. (*Horwich and Westhoughton Journal*)

The Palace Cinema, in Church Street, in September 1947. Caterpillars had invaded the cinema, beginning life in an adjoining field, where they stripped kale to the stalks. Mr Ferguson, the manager, said they were under the eaves and even in the operating box. Other parts of Westhoughton were apparently also 'crawling', and the phenomenon was attributed to dry weather and the fact that there were fewer birds, due to the previous severe winter. (photograph courtesy of *Horwich and Westhoughton Journal*)

The interior, in 1947. The cinema was popularly known as the Rink, having been a skating rink before it was a cinema. There was also a billiard hall at the rear. With two cinemas competing for custom, one way of attracting customers was to arrange for local events to be filmed. In 1930, the film taken of the British Legion Garden Fete and Fair held on 19 July was shown at the cinema. In the 1930s, when a familiar question would have been 'artut pitchers neet?', Bolton had twenty-eight cinemas and Westhoughton had two. The cinema closed in 1956.

Oaklea, Bolton Road, was the home of Robert Shaw, the film star and author, who was born in King Street, Westhoughton, in August 1927. He was the son of Dr Thomas Shaw, who came to Westhoughton as assistant to Dr W.D. Hatton, who was on duty at the Pretoria Pit. Dr Hatton died a few months later and Dr Shaw took over the practice, moving into Hatton's residence and surgery. Robert went to the White Horse Church of England Infants School, and his father enjoyed drinking with the locals at the Rose and Crown opposite. Although he only lived in Westhoughton until he was seven, when his family moved to the Orkneys, one of his earliest recollections was of mill workers clattering past his home in their clogs, singing while he was still in bed.

Robert Shaw died in August 1978, and in 1996, to celebrate 100 years of the cinema, a plaque commemorating his connection with Westhoughton was put on the wall of the Town Hall. His first major film part was in *The Dambusters* and many others followed, including, *A Man For All Seasons*, and *Jaws*. His first novel, *The Hiding Place*, was published in 1959, and his second, *The Sun Doctor*, won The Hawthornden Prize for literature.

Carnival and Gala, 1924. Before the war the Gala Sports and Rose Queen Carnival, held on the Red Lion Ground, and organized by the Westhoughton Sick Nursing Association was a major event, with a procession throughout the town. The sports were of a high standard, and recognised as such for miles around. The Westhoughton Joint Friendly Societies were also involved and the event, as well as providing a great day out to be looked forward to all year, raised lots of money for charity. This carnival was said to be reminiscent of pre-war carnivals and one notable feature was that it was 'free from the vulgarity and inane effects that have marked numerous recent affairs of this sort'. A feature of many galas were 'the silent twins', who went around challenging people to make them smile.

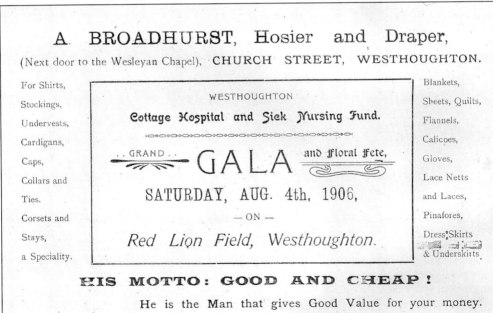

Advertisement, 1906.

Carnival, August 1924, organized by the Chequerbent and White Horse Schools, and held at Taylor Park. From left to right, back row: W. Seddon, T. Crippin, Adrian Baxter, J. Wilkinson (father of Jan Holden, TV actress). Front row: Miss M. Calverley, Miss R. Coop, Miss E. Leyland (teacher at Chequerbent School), Miss K.M. Leyland (headmistress at the Parochial School), -?-. Miss Coop, Miss Calverley, and Miss Ruth Crippin all taught at the White Horse School. Standing in the background in the top hat is Mr Harold Taylor. In addition to the fancy dress competition, there were decorated lorries, including a live cow, representing 'keaw yed', and a model of a colliery. The evening sports were not completed because of rain, but were adjourned to be completed on the following Wednesday. Of the collected proceeds 75% went to charities and the Bolton Infirmary, and the remainder to the two schools. (photograph courtesy of B. Clare)

The Fair, 24 August 1976. Westhoughton wakes attracted huge crowds at one time with special excursion trains from Bolton. The wakes is really a religious festival, traditionally falling on Bartlemass, commemorating the dedication of the local church, and is linked with the parish church of Saint Bartholomew, and in the past, with Deane church. Wakes weekend is the weekend after 23 August, commemorating the festival of St Bartholomew, unless that date falls on a Sunday, in which case it is that weekend. The wakes were associated in the past with a rush bearing, the custom of putting rushes over the church floor after a procession. There was much merry making and feasting and vast quantities of wakes pasties were consumed. Ditchfield's Old English Customs Extant at the Present Time (1896) mentions 'a huge pie made in the shape of a cow's head, which is eaten on the day of the Wake'. The pie has gone, replaced by oval shaped pasties. In 1960, 36 dozen pasties were sold in a single night in one pub. (photograph courtesy of *Horwich and Westhoughton Journal*)

The Wakes Entertainment in aid of the School Funds.

THE WESTHOUGHTON HISTRIONIC CLUB WILL GIVE A

DRAMATIC ENTERTAINMENT

On the Wakes Monday, August 28th, 1876,

The proceeds of which will go to the School Fund.

It is hoped that the Entertainment will be successful in every respect, and that the Club will be able to hand over to the Treasurer of the School a handsome surplus.

The following Programme will be gone through:

D'YE KNOW ME NOW.

A Farce—In one Act—Two Scenes.

NOGO DUMPS—"A Doleful Commercial" ... ... Mr. CHARLES BOULTON.
SEPTIMUS SELLWELL JOLLY—"A Commercial, jolly by name and jolly by nature"
Mr. JESSE WHITTLE.
JABEZ SNIGGINS—"A Grocer" ... ... Mr. GEORGE GRUNDY.
SAMUEL WAITWELL—"A Waiter" ... ... Mr. J. W. BOULTON.

SCENE 1st—A Room in an Inn. 2nd—Interior of Grocer's Shop.

SCENES IN THE STUDIO.

A Darkey Drama—In one Act.

Mr. FELIX GRUMBO—"From the country" ... ... Mr. JAMES HARTLEY.
Mr. COLLODION—"A Photographer" ... ... Mr. C. E. SCOTT.
ADOLPHUS—"A boy up at-all-fuss" ... ... Mr. GEORGE HANSON.

SCENE—Interior of Photographic Studio.

THE VIRGINIA MUMMY.

A Negro Farce—In one Act—Two Scenes.

GINGER BLUE—"A Negro Waiter" ... ... Mr. CHARLES BOULTON.
Dr. GALEN ... ... Mr. FERGUS DOBBIE.
CAPTAIN RIFLE ... ... Mr. C. E. SCOTT.
CHARLES ... ... Mr. JAMES GRUNDY.
O'LEARY ... ... Mr. J. W. BOULTON.
LUCY ... ... Mr. J. R. HEWITT.

SCENE 1st—Room in Hotel. 2nd—Dr. Galen's Surgery.

TO CONCLUDE WITH DANCING.

Mr. BENSON'S STRING BAND, of Wigan, has been engaged to attend, and will play selections of music during the intervals of the programme, as well as for Dancing, which will commence about 9 o'clock.

PRICES OF ADMISSION:

Reserved Seats, numbered, 1s. 6d., to be had only from the Misses Platt, where a plan may be seen. Second Seats, 1s., to be had from the Members of the Club.

No reduced price of Admission during the evening. Doors open at 6.30 p.m., to commence at 7 prompt.
Carriages may be ordered for 11 p.m.

Wakes, Monday 28 August 1876

Associated with the Wakes is Westhoughton's 'keaw yed' legend, a simple story of a farmer and a cow. A cow got its head stuck in a gate. A farmer came along. Faced with the cow and gate problem, he solved it by sawing off the cow's head. The story has similar variations world wide, and indicates stupidity, but also the Howfeners ability to laugh at themselves, allowing themselves to be nicknamed 'keaw yeds'. The story had never been heard of before 1870, and is said to derive from an incorrect newspaper story, rather than a real legend. In all the depictions of cow's heads in Westhoughton none were in conjunction with a gate. One explanation of the keaw yed legend relates to the old handloom weavers, who each week used to walk to Leigh with thin lengths of cloth which they sold to merchants. Their silhouetted appearance in the distance apparently resembled cows heads, and led to the nickname. (photograph courtesy of *Horwich and Westhoughton Journal*)

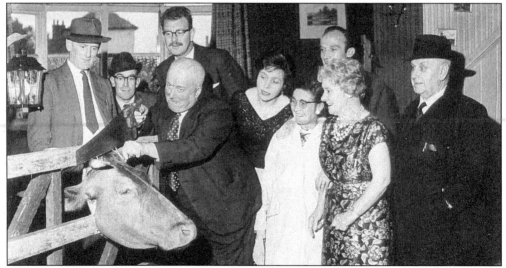

Red Lion, 1962. The brewers encouraged the 'keaw yed' story. The cow's head was usually adorned with ribbons and flowers, mostly marigolds and parsley with one or two gigantic loaves of jannock. Another explanation of the nickname is that an ox was roasted to celebrate the victory of the Battle of Waterloo in 1815, and a mock battle took place for the honour of owning the head, between people from Daisy Hill and those from the town centre. The victors were dubbed 'keaw yeds' by the losers. Also Westhoughton passed through hard times in the 1830s and 1840s and it was the custom to have cows head broth for Sunday dinner. Families clubbed together to buy the head. The cow's head represents the endurance of the people in very hard times, hence the nickname. (photograph courtesy of *Bolton Evening News*)

Local holidaymakers at Douglas, Isle of Man, in July 1947. Many Westhoughton people still took the traditional holiday week, but it no longer meant a complete exodus from the town, as many worked in areas with different holiday patterns, such as Leigh. The boat train for Douglas was the most popular of the Friday evening specials, and Mr S.E. Jones, the Westhoughton stationmaster reported that the Isle of Man was the most popular destination. In 1938, 'terms' at a small hotel in Douglas were from 8s 6d a week. (photograph courtesy of *Horwich and Westhoughton Journal*)

Sixty 'necessitous children' from Westhoughton are at Westhoughton station en route to Conway, North Wales for a holiday on 7 September 1937. The money was raised by a wireless appeal by Rhys Davies MP, and they were joined by 120 children from Hindley, Blackrod and Aspull. The whole of this area was hit by unemployment, and times were very hard, but as a result of Rhys Davies' efforts these children had a holiday to remember. On the right is Mr J.G. Hindley, who was in charge. How pleased he must have been next morning at 6.00 a.m. when most of them were up and awake, and asking to go to the beach. (photograph courtesy of *Horwich and Westhoughton Journal*)

Rigby and Sons, garage and charabanc proprietors, of No. 30 Church Lane, 1932. Charabancs often only had passenger seats at the weekend, as the vehicle reverted to haulage duties during the week. The seats were constructed in such a way as to give each person an elevated view for 'rubber necking'. Early 'charas' were not fast. In 1917, Arthur Christy, a Bolton motor coach proprietor, was fined £10 and 1½ guineas costs, for speeding at seventeen miles an hour, but it was good advertising and it brought him £60 worth of business. When it rained the unwieldy covers could not be put on quickly, and if you were caught in a storm you knew about it. The seats were hard, the engines overheated, and the passengers were often thirsty, so there were plenty of stops at Ye Olde Inn. Blackpool was a long trip and the first 'chara' to attempt a half-day trip to the resort got a grand send-off from Victoria Square in May 1921. The fare was 11s 6d then, but by 1937 the standard charge was 5s.

Westhoughton Agricultural Show in 1949. The first show after the war was held on Saturday 20 September 1947, on land at the White Horse. Later venues included, Ormstons Farm, Wingates Lane, Barr Fold Farm, Chorley Road, Snydale Hall Farm, and Hulton Park. In 1949, as well as the usual competitions and events, there was also a display of rayon goods sponsored by the British Rayon Federation, 'at a cost, which to the ordinary individual is staggering'. Another attraction was the famous dog 'Beauty', winner of the Animals VC for the rescue of sixty-three animals during the London blitz in 1940-1941. The last one was in 1959, and the balance of £500 was given to ten local charities. (photograph courtesy of *Horwich and Westhoughton Journal*)

Cattle fair. The Cattle Fair on 13 October 1875 was the eightieth one held for horned cattle, horses, pigs, etc. and took place in Westhoughton Cricket Club field, near the Red Lion. There were forty-four entries but less visitors than the previous year. The judges were Mr Wilson, of Masongill Hall, Yorks., Mr Whitehead of Wheelton, and Mr W. Langton of Park Hall, Blackrod. Prizes ranged from £1 to 10s

Ploughing and Hedging Competition, 1939. This was held at Reeves House Farm, just off the A6 near the Fourgates Hotel. The chief award went to John Dixon of Billingham-on-Tees, Durham, the Champion of the UK. Competitions began in 1936 and were also held at Hart Common farm and Brinsop Hall Farm. Prizes were awarded for various categories of ploughing and hedging expertise, the special prize for the best ridge being a pig trough, valued at 15s. A power driven double furrow plough was demonstrated at this event, prompting the question, 'Will the farmer's team soon be a thing of the past?' (photograph courtesy of *Horwich and Westhoughton Journal*)

Stakes were provided for the hedging competition, which the rules stipulated, must be used. There was a silver challenge cup, presented by H.O. Dixon, for the best hedger living within a radius of fifteen miles of Westhoughton Town Hall. Hart Common Farm, the venue in December 1945 was farmed by Jim Walker, who was a family descendant of Robert Walker, one of three brothers who came from Scotland to seek their fortune – walking all the way. Peter went to Warrington and founded Walker's Brewery; William founded Walker's Tannery in Bolton, and Robert set up as a farmer in Westhoughton. Jim's prowess with heavy horses and the plough are described by Barry Cockcroft in *The Princes of the Plough*, Dent, 1978. (photograph courtesy of *Horwich and Westhoughton Journal*)

'Upon the ploughman much of the success of the crop depends' – a young competitor around 1940. The ploughs used had to be swing or wheel, and no lines or marks were to be used. Competitors were allowed to use five pegs with assistance to set them and pick them up. (photograph courtesy of *Horwich and Westhoughton Journal*)

Westhoughton Public Brass Band, c. 1900. The band originated in the Daisy Hill area and the band are in front of Pendlebury's Farm, later owned by Paul Barlow and situated off Park Road, between Leigh Road and Hall Lee Park. Mr John Crompton joined the band at the age of twelve and in the picture are his father Henry and brothers Nathan, Joseph and William. The conductor was Joseph Chadwick. Others in the picture are farmer Jim Pendlebury and his son Jim, Dick and Jack Gaskell, George and Shadrach Chadwick, Henry and Frank Hodkinson, Fred Hindley, Shadrach Hootson, John Green, Billy Cockshout, Eddy Powell, and Fred Hingley. In the 1930s they practised in a hut behind the Cross Guns.

Westhoughton Old Prize Band, 1920. The brass band movement originated in the early part of the nineteenth century and was traditionally strong in the North of England, resulting in the formation of thousands of brass bands, the Old Band being founded in 1854. The first event they played a part in was the celebration of the end of the Crimean War in 1856. When the old factory chimney opposite the White Lion was struck by lightning and then rebuilt, they played on the top, although some members of the band refused this opportunity. In 1869 there was a grand draw to raise money for uniforms. Prizes were a harmonium, a fat pig, a sack of flour, a cheese, an iron bedstead, and a fat duck. They threw out a challenge to friends in the rival community in Wingates, and the rest, as they say, is history!

Wingates Temperance Band, 1910. Wingates Band was formed in 1873 by members of the Bible Class of Wingates Independent Methodist church, after taunts from their friends in the Old Band. The original name of the drum and fife band they formed was Westhoughton Good Templars, but within a year they switched to brass, and in 1878 the name was changed to Wingates Temperance Band, a name that lasted until 1980, when the word 'temperance' was dropped. They were just like any other band at first, performing locally at concerts, walking days, and civic processions, until 1891 when money was raised to buy quality instruments, and the band signed its first professional conductor, Mr William Rimmer, of Southport, 'the man who made Wingates Band world famous'. By the turn of the century he had turned Wingates into one of Britain's top brass bands, and in 1906, the Band achieved national fame by winning the 'double', namely the British Open and the British National Championships. The following year they did it again, the first band to achieve this feat, which has been repeated only once in subsequent years by the Black Dyke Mills Band. They could have toured the continent and America, but preferred to work as miners and play music as a hobby. This triumph was followed by tragedy when in December 1910 they lost half of their members and their chairman, Mr W. Cowburn (the secretary), and famous soprano soloist Mr E. Lonsdale, in the Pretoria Pit Disaster. The postcard is dated 7 July 1910, 6 months before the tragedy. This terrible loss was difficult to recover from, but they did, and in 1915 recorded their first record, A Military Church Parade/3rd Dragoon Guards March, for the Regal Records label on a 10 inch shellac disc, the first of over 150 recordings. In 1931 they were world champions, returning to Westhoughton on Monday and were back at work on Tuesday. Eighteen of the 27 band members worked in the pit and most started work at 5.00 a.m. 'The manager, Mr Ramsden Whitwam, works on his back all day in a space 18 inches high, and after work manages and plays in a world class band. *That's the stuff Wingates are made of*'. This internationally renowned band, one of the best brass bands of all time, has won over 18 championships to date and has been in the final of the British Open 87 times. Its fabulous history is currently being researched and Wingates memorabilia, particularly photographs, memories, and anecdotes are sought. The supporters club has over 700 members and the band's headquarters are at Wingates Square, Westhoughton, BL5 3PS.

Sydney Ratcliffe in 1974 with the recording of the test piece 'Honour and Glory', when the band won first prize in the Crystal Palace championships in 1931. This elusive copy was given to the band by the Besses o' th' Barn band. Syd was born at No. 1 Queen Street, on 29 March 1905. His mother Emma was a silk weaver at Chadwick's silk mill and his father was employed at the Pretoria Pit. He worked part-time at Taylor and Hartley's mill and then full-time at the Starkie Colliery. He played for Westhoughton Cricket Club, making his debut aged fourteen, (see p.14). He joined the police force and later worked as a director in the textile industry. He had a lifelong love of brass band music and a lifelong association with Wingates. As a boy he worked as a gardener for Mr Dixon, the mine owner, who was president of the band and their greatest benefactor. Syd himself became president in 1973 and in 1976 was elected honorary life vice-president, the only such appointment in its 100 years existence. Read Syd's life story in *From Little Brass to Big Brass*, by Leslie Chapples. (photograph courtesy of *Horwich and Westhoughton Journal*)

Advertisement, 1931.

Houghton Weavers. The Houghton Weavers recently celebrated twenty-five years in showbusiness, living up to their catchphrase 'keep folk smiling'. The original members were Denis Littler, Norman Prince, Tony Berry, and David Littler. They got together in 1975 when Norman Prince, who had been involved in folk groups for years, met Tony Berry, a singer in the local social clubs. Soon they teamed up with brothers, Denis and David Littler, and within three years they had their own series on television, entitled *Sit Thi Deawn*. In an interview in the Radio Times, Norman said, 'Westhoughton hasn't changed much in the last fifty years, but it's expanding, becoming a dormitory town. We don't want to get on by expanding: we get on with things in Westhoughton by standing still! We've already got here what most people are striving for - a sense of community - and we want to keep it. (photograph courtesy of *Bolton Evening News*.)

Howfen Weavers. The Houghton Weavers took their name from the weaving history of the town. These women and girls worked in a Westhoughton Mill, around 1920. They have their long hair up for safety.

Seven

Sport

'To play well, to win well, and if fate deems it, to lose well'

Westhoughton Cricket Club motto

Ethel Johnson of Lord Street, Westhoughton, ran for Bolton United Harriers. She trained as a teacher at Edge Hill College and in 1927, aged eighteen, she won the first of her six Northern Counties 100 yards Championships. She first represented England in 1931 and in 1932 won the English 100 yards championships in 11 seconds, breaking the world record for that distance, an achievement that was not really officially recognised because about that time the official distance was changed from yards to metres. Her ambition was to do even better in the Olympic games but it was not to be, sustaining an injury which she put down to overtraining on an unsuitable practice track. After the Olympics she received a letter from the Women's Amateur Athletic Association thanking her for her services and saying, 'we all know you had extremely bad luck but you at least have the consolation of upholding British prestige and the fact you are a good loser.' She retired in 1935 aged twenty-six, preferring to finish when still running well rather than fade out gradually. Ethel taught at Kearsley West School from 1929-1935, Westhoughton Council Junior from 1938-1945, and was headmistress of the County School, Stalmine, in the Fylde, from 1945-1964. She died on 3 April 1964, aged fifty-five, while visiting her home town. She was widely respected, and 'infused new life and brought scholastic success to her village school'.

Cllrs Selby, Berry, and Harry Shaw at Trinity Street station, Bolton, wishing bon voyage and good luck to Ethel Johnson, who was leaving for the Olympic Games in Los Angeles on 12 July 1932. Ethel's parents are on her right, and behind her, on her left, is her brother-in-law, Bob Floyd. She is carrying a silver-plated horseshoe, made by Mr J. Rigby the blacksmith, out of the metal which once belonged to a bell in the Westhoughton parish church belfry. It was decorated with a red rose, and red, white, and blue ribbons. Cllr Shaw, just before the train left, wished Miss Johnson good luck and expressed the hope that 'she might bring further honour to her country, her town, and herself.' Miss Johnson replied: 'Thank you. If I don't it won't be because I didn't try.' She sailed to America on the *Empress of Britain*, which also carried British Government representatives, including Stanley Baldwin and Lord Hailsham, to the Ottawa conference. Unfortunately, Ethel suffered an injury in training and as a result did not qualify in her heat in the 100 metres. She was however greeted by hundreds of people when she returned, being met at Four Lane Ends by Mr R.J. Davies MP, the Rose Queen, and representatives of Bolton Harriers. At Chequerbent the Westhoughton Old Band played her into town where she was greeted by hundreds of people. (photograph courtesy of *Horwich and Westhoughton Journal*)

Walking race, c. 1900. The walkers are proceeding down Market Street, having just passed the White Lion Public House. Foot racing', or 'pedestrianism' had a long tradition and attracted large crowds, as well as heavy backing from publicans, sporting gentlemen and gamblers. On race days crowds would line the course, usually between 100 yards and a mile long. Bolton's most famous 'pedestrian' was a weaver, Ben Hart, whose feats could empty the town's mills for half a day as crowds flocked to watch. One Monday in 1834 he raced against the famous 'mountain stag' from Belmont, before a crowd of 5,000 on Kersal Moor.

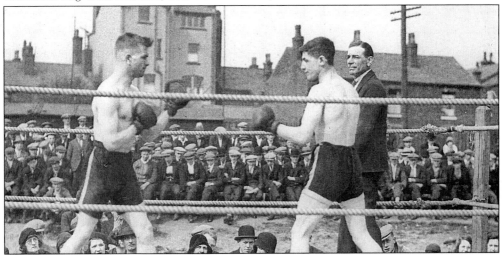

Boxing match on the Red Lion Football Ground on 29 July 1932. The boxing ring was kept in G. Birtles' workshop and was used by Westhoughton Lads Club, whose headquarters was the Wheatsheaf Hotel on Market Street. Jack Lord used to train the boys. On this occasion the contests were advertised as 'better than last time', and consisted of four bouts. The main contest was Jimmy Chadwick of Wingates v. Joe Heathcote of Farnworth, who was thought to be the best boy in Bolton. Also fighting were Jim O'Toole and Ernie Harrison, 'two sparkling fighters from gong to gong.' The fight between Billy Haycock, of Chew Moor, 'Westhoughton's Kid Berg,' and Pobhy Young, of Manchester, was 'worth going a long way to see'. Admission was 6d for men and 2d for ladies and boys. The spectators in the ringside seats paid 1s for the privilege. The referee was Alf Brooks of Horwich.

The Westhoughton Charity Cup Final, May 1947. Cllr Howarth presents the trophy to Jones, captain of Aspull Youth Club, who beat the Stag and Griffin 1-0 (the scorer was Holding). George Twist, Westhoughton's first class referee, is on the left. Thirty-eight teams took part, raising £200 for charity. There were 5,000 spectators crammed into the Red Lion Ground and the *Journal* described the atmosphere, 'the Charity Cup Final at the Red Lion Ground is more than a football match, it is an occasion, a Wembley in miniature. Long before the match, spectators were pouring into the town centre from Chequerbent and Aspull, and special transport helped carry the fans. The British Legion Band paraded Market Street, prior to providing a short entertainment on the field. Aspull supporters were flamboyant, with ex-ARP rattles adding their quota to the general medley of sound. Then came the roar heralding the arrival of the teams, accompanied by the Football League and international referee, Mr W.H. Evans of Liverpool.' In addition, the committee arranged a special match, between Aspull Youth Club, Charity Cup Winners, and Lomax's XI, Bolton Royal Infirmary cup winners, which raised £50 to help those involved in the disaster at Burnden Park in March 1946. The Charity Cup was originally organized by 'the friendly societies' to help their members financially, and Westhoughton Olympic were the first winners in 1893. At the end of the First World War, control was handed over to the Westhoughton Football League, which was founded in 1917 at Dearden's Temperance Bar. Matches were played at Taylor Park, and later, at The Red Lion Field. The trophy is very special, once hotly competed for at a time when every area of the district had a team in the local league, which had three divisions. The matches were always well attended and watched by large crowds. The Tonge Cup final played on Good Friday and the Charity Cup at the end of the season were the highlights. The Charity Cup went into retirement during the Second World War, and was revived soon afterwards. In the 1950s soccer in the town hit the doldrums. The league and the Charity Cup, (after a brief flirtation with rugby), went out of existence. It was revived in 1969 and funds were augmented by a big cabaret night. In 1973 this was held at Blighty's Club in Farnworth and Tommy Cooper topped the bill. Instrumental in the revival were George Twist, Peter James, Bill Cartwright, Brian Fray, and treasurer Ben Johnson. Little Hulton were the winners in 1995-1996, when the cup was last competed for. (photograph courtesy of *Horwich and Westhoughton Journal*)

Charity Cup Final, Friday, 23 April 1948. Tempest United (in white) *v.* Reform Club (stripes). Arthur Leigh, second from the left, was the referee and the linesmen were T.H. Cooper and H. Tootill. Between the teams are George Twist and C.R. Mountford, New Zealand and Wigan Rugby Club international, and his wife. Tempest United won 1-0 and C.R. Mountford presented the cup and individual trophies, congratulating the winning team, whose captain thanked Reform Club for a clean sporting game. A crowd of 4,000 raised £200 for charity. (photograph courtesy of *Horwich and Westhoughton Journal*)

Chequerbent Football Club, in the 1922-1923 season. Their nickname was 'the midgets'. The longest ever local football match took place on Good Friday, 18 April 1919 between Dobb Brow and Chequerbent, and was a cup semi-final lasting 4 hours 55 minutes. The match, played on the ground of Westhoughton Collieries, was 0-0 after 90 minutes and both captains got the agreement of the referee and league officials to play to the finish. The match kicked off at 10.30 a.m and the golden goal came at 3.25pm.

Wigan Road Villa FC, the Cup Final, 25 March 1948. Fred Southern, captain of Wigan Road Villa, receives the Westhoughton Football Challenge Cup from George Twist after leading his team to victory on Good Friday morning. George Twist from Church Street, Westhoughton was the referee for the fourth round FA Cup tie between Chelsea and Plymouth Argyle, on the first Saturday after King George V died on Monday, 20 January 1936. George played amateur football until he had to give up after being wounded in 1915. He worked as a colliery clerk, and in 1922 became secretary to Coppull Central, then a semi-professional football club. In 1924 he took up refereeing, moving up the ladder to the Football League in 1932. He was a great supporter of local football and was elected to the Lancashire Football Association Council in 1945. He was the longest serving member when he died in 1976. He was a sidesman at Westhoughton parish church for thirty-five years. (photograph courtesy of *Horwich and Westhoughton Journal*)

International footballer, Jack Bruton, was born in Westhoughton on 21 November 1903, and was a miner before becoming a professional footballer. He played for Hart Common, in the Westhoughton Sunday School League, and Hindley Green in the Lancashire Alliance, before signing amateur forms for Bolton Wanderers, where he played for the 'A' team. He went to Horwich RMI, and was signed by Burnley in March 1925, for £125. He was transferred to Blackburn Rovers in December 1929 for £6,500, the record at that time being £8,000. A goalscoring outside right, he played for England against France and Belgium in 1928, and received his International Cap against Scotland in April 1929. He also played for the Football League against the Irish League in 1928, and against the Scottish League in 1934. He was also an excellent cricketer, and was one of the opening batsmen for Westhoughton Cricket Club. He retired from playing during the Second World War, after 491 league games, and was manager of Blackburn from 1947-1949, and Bournemouth from 1950-1956. After this he worked for a lamp company. He died on 13 March 1986.

A 'gam' lad. Francis Lee was born in Westhoughton on 29 April 1944, and went to Westhoughton Boys Secondary Modern, and later to Horwich Technical College. He played for his school team in the morning, and for Winrow's in the Bolton Boys Federation in the afternoon. Frank Tomlinson, and Bill Brookes, Federation Secretary and chairman, could tell straight away that this small blond lad was 'more than a bit special'. He won a place in the Horwich and Westhoughton Schools team and was the star in the Mid-Lancashire Schools Cup Final on 10 May 1958. He is on the front row, second from the left. Chased by a number of clubs, he signed for Bolton Wanderers, and made a sensational debut, aged sixteen, against Manchester City on 5 November 1960. Veteran player Harry Nuttall's verdict, 'as a player he's what we always called 'gam', and that sort always has a chance.'

With Malcolm Allison at the Westhoughton Charity Cup Final, on Sunday 23 April 1972, this was the first time the final had been played on a Sunday. Francis was the president. He also played cricket for the Westhoughton third team, and in the same week that he made his debut for Wanderers, he received the batting, bowling and catching prizes. He continued to play cricket in the Bolton League, like many other footballing names, and on the day of the World Cup Final in 1966, was playing for Heaton against Bradshaw. Four years later he was playing for England in the World Cup in Mexico. He signed for Manchester City in 1967, and later played for Derby County, winning 27 caps for England. A very successful businessman, he lived in Westhoughton until 1978, when he moved to Cheshire. (photograph courtesy of *Bolton Evening News*)

Westhoughton Cricket Club, 1923. Players from left to right, back row: T. Vickers, A. Hurst, Sydney Ratcliffe, F. Gerrard. Second row: left with the Homburg hat is Benjamin Withington. Other players: P. Peet, T. Nuttall, W. Johnson (large cap). Front row: W. Hurst, H. Pollard, S. Heyes, Dr R.C. Racker, (captain), H.O. Dixon (president of Wingates Temperance Band, and general manager of Westhoughton Coal and Cannel Company and Starkie Collieries), P. Gerrard, and Ralph Hurst (professional). The motto of the club is to 'play well, to win well, and if fate deems it, to lose well'. The club is thought to have originated in 1856, but although no early records were kept, a centenary was duly celebrated in 1956.

FAMOUS LOCAL CRICKETERS.

RALPH HURST,
Who has been re-engaged as professional to the Westhoughton
Club, is one of the many capable cricketers reared at Daisy Hi
Made his name as seductive left-arm bowler.

PRESTONS FOR CHOICE GIFTS.

Raph Hurst, the professional, in 1923. This postcard was issued by Prestons of Bolton. In 1864, the team was attached to the Albion Mill at Wingates, and then became the Westhoughton Royal Cricket Club, playing on a field adjoining the vicarage. In 1875 cricket was promoted 'to keep young men from public houses and gaming'. After losing their ground in 1879 the club broke up until it was reformed in 1883, after a new field was acquired. In the 1920s and 1930s the club grew stronger, helped by the development of players such as the Tyldesley brothers. In 1945 the club became owners of the ground, then known as Bromilow Park, and renamed it after this great cricketing family.

The plaque dedicated to the Tyldesleys was unveiled on 24 August 1945, and the ground was renamed. Harry, William, James and Richard Tyldesley were the sons of James Tyldesley, and all four played for Lancashire. 'Owd Jim', their father, played for Hart Common and after living in Carlisle, came back to Westhoughton in the 1890s. He had a major influence on his sons, and had a religious attitude to cricket saying, 'I believe it is the duty of the Church to teach people to play the game.' Young Jim died aged only thirty-two in 1923 after a minor operation. He had been on the Lancashire ground staff since 1913, and it was said that 'the County of Lancashire had no better fast bowler for seven years and does not know how to fill his boots'. Harry died in 1935, and like his brother William played for the county before the First World War. The most well-known though was Richard. 'Our Dick', was one of the things Westhoughton was famous for. Dick was born in 1897, and played for Lancashire from 1919-1931, taking 1,449 wickets. He played one test match against Australia in 1930, and was presented with a beautiful timepiece and a silver cigarette case by the Westhoughton Council – he was the first cricketer from Westhoughton to represent his country. He was a superb fielder and bowler despite his ample bulk. He was the landlord of the Dog and Pheasant (see p. 101). He died in September 1943, but his rosy red face continues to shine out from pavilion photographs at Old Trafford. A framed report in the library celebrates Dick's achievement in the 1924 Roses match when Yorkshire were all out for 33 runs, 'our Dick' taking 6 wickets. Westhoughton Cricket Club prides itself on supplying more cricketers to the county than any other club in Lancashire. Others were Dick Pollard, nicknamed 'th'owd chainhorse', who played from 1933-1950, and four times for England, William Farrimond, and more recently Michael Watkinson. (photograph courtesy of *Bolton Evening News*)

New Rock Farm, Blundells Farm, with Daisy Hill church in the background. Daisy Hill Cricket and Tennis Club was founded in 1896 and the original ground was at Bellhouse Hartwell, off Leigh Road. In 1911 land was purchased at St James Street, which had a farmstead with a duck pond. The pavilion is built on the farmhouse site above, and the car park at the rear of the pavilion was the duck pond.

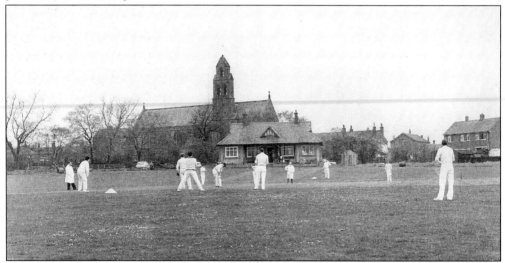

Daisy Hill Cricket Club, St James Street, c. 1970. The ground and original clubhouse were presented to the club by Mr Wardle, left in trust by him on behalf of his wife, the daughter of Thomas Walsh, owner of Greenvale Print and Dye Works. They are one of the oldest members of the Bolton and District Cricket Association, having joined in 1905. Over the years many players of international quality, such as Billy Farrimond, Dick Pollard and Dick Naylor have been born in or played for Daisy Hill. Billy Farrimond played for Lancashire from 1924-1945, and made four test appearances, and like Dick Pollard also played for Westhoughton, as well as Lancashire and England.

The club is a focus for the Daisy Hill community. In January 1965 a new clinic was opened in the clubhouse, saving a long and arduous pram push up the hill to Westhoughton, in the days when prams were prams! (photograph courtesy of *Bolton Evening News*)

Westhoughton Golf Club founder members, taken at the Grange, the home of H.O. Dixon. The club was officially opened on 29 September 1934 by Mr W.R. Gregson, captain of Hesketh Golf Club, and a director of the Westhoughton Coal and Cannel Company. The club was originally known as the British Legion Golf Club, opened in 1930, but when the lease ran out in March 1934 it was decided to form a new club on land at Long Island Farm, which was owned by the Westhoughton Coal and Cannel Company. Cllr Hilton, chairman of the council, and not a golfer, said he was amazed by the astonishing transformation of the farm into a golf course. Mr J. Ackers, president of the club, welcomed Mr A. Critchley who was president of the English Golf Union, and said that after being honoured by the presence of such eminent golf officials, Westhoughton would definitely be on the map.

Wingates Cycling Club, c. 1928. Inter Club Meet, Mount Crescent, Fleetwood. In August 1928, ten of these members took part in a 24-hour endurance test, setting off from Westhoughton Town Hall at 6 p.m on a Saturday night – they were in Lancaster for a 9 p.m. supper. 'In the dim glow of cycle lamps we followed the Lune for some distance before turning left for Kirkby Lonsdale. Our noisy motoring brethren had long since left us, and to the hum of our tyres, the chatter of our own voices, with here and there a singsong, we pedalled and glided into Windermere. Ambleside, Rydal and Grasmere gave us eerie glimpses off the silent lakes. Night is not the best time to see these places, but in the silence, unbroken except for the whirr of our own wheels, the experience was pleasant and worth the trouble.'

Wingates Cycling Club, August 1949. H. Callaghan, the winner of their annual twenty-five mile competition is in the centre. The club probably had their origins in the Westhoughton Clarion Cycling Club. The national Clarion Cycling Club began in 1894, and originated from *The Clarion* newspaper, a penny Socialist weekly, founded by Robert Blatchford. Cycling grew rapidly in popularity in the 1890s and local clubs were formed in all parts of the country. In Gems of Thought, a keepsake from the bazaar held in the Carnegie Hall in December 1909, a Clarion writer, contributes the following, 'Don't be too ready to bow down to any doctrine or authority simply because they are 'respectable' or your cap will always be in your hand, and your knees always baggy.' The Bolton Clarion Cycling Club still flourishes. Read more in *Fellowship is Life*. Denis Pye, Clarion Publishing, 1995.

Eight

Streets

Odd names, Bawfern Fowt to Old Sirs

The front of Nos 1 and 2 Balfern Fold, 1935. Known as 'Bawfern Fowt', an old lady who had lived here for sixty years stopped paying the rent because she said, 'I've paid fer't house six times over'. The cottages were subject to a clearance order in 1935. Westhoughton has more than its share of odd names, such as Alick's Fold, The Pungle, Radical Nursery (the highest point in Westhoughton), Fish Fold Farm, Top'o'th' Slack, and many more.

Houses adjoining the Rose and Crown, Bolton Road, 1935. A proposal to turn the two houses into a storage house for the adjacent public house, rather than demolish them, was agreed to by the Minister of Health.

Cow Lees Farm, behind the Rose and Crown, 1974. Bolton Road was known as Cow Lee-lane. On the west side of Bolton Road, behind Oaklea, and south of Manchester Road was Warcock Hill, the site of a battle on Westhoughton Common on 15 December 1642. When Civil War broke out in that year between Charles I and the Parliamentarians, Lancashire was divided, with the west of the county tending to be Catholic and Royalist, and the east, including Bolton and Manchester, being Parliamentarians. At Warcock Hill three companies of Parliamentarians met 1,000 horse and foot of Royalists who were garrisoned at Wigan, and a battle ensued. The 3 companies were taken prisoner, and the three captains went to Lord Derby's home at Lathom. The defeat was a 'great grief and discouragement to the Parliament party'. A mural depicting the battle was painted above the Market Hall in 1987. The area is now a housing development, but beware of ghosts for they have been seen, including a sighting by one person, who unaware of the history of the area, reported seeing a ghostly re-enactment of the battle.

The New Inn, No. 590 Chorley Road, 1964. The landlord of the New Inn in 1870 was James Ainscough, and in 1896 was William Beatty. The New Inn became the Brinsop Arms. (photograph courtesy of *General Electric Company*)

Outside the Dog and Pheasant, Chorley Road, 1957. It was built in 1762, first called the Dog Inn, and was always a large public house. In 1854 it was for sale and described as having three parlours, a tap room, club-room, bar, three bedrooms, two cellars, brew house, malt room, piggery, garden, cottage and shippon. The pub was known as the Dog and Pheasant from the early nineteenth century, and was rebuilt in 1901. Dick Tyldesley, the Lancashire and England cricketer was the landlord in the 1930s and early 1940s. In modern times this large and popular pub has had various names, Amigos, Loose Goose, Rosie O'Grady's, and Leo's. (photograph courtesy of *Bolton Evening News*)

Advertisement for Dog and Pheasant, 1930.

Church Street. This postcard was sent from Westhoughton to Somerset and postmarked 8.30 p.m. on the 28 August 1906. It was originally called Chapel Lane, but the name was changed after the parish church was built in 1870. Opposite the church, No. 2 Church Street, now the 'Casa Nostra' restaurant, was once the Grapes Inn.

102

Advertisements, 1897.

Dickinsons Yard at Wellington Street, Charles Street and James Street was proposed as a children's playground around 1962. (photograph courtesy of *Bolton Evening News*)

Leigh Road, 1935, when the property was considered unfit for human habitation by the Minister of Health.

Daisy Hill Lodge, Leigh Road. Mr W. Booth's fathers house, now demolished, was near the entrance to the Print Works.

White Lion Inn and the post office, c. 1908. In the early part of the nineteenth century it was the place appointed for receiving letters and the room on the left side of the front door was set apart as a post office. The custom was to place the letters in the window, suitable racks having been made to accommodate them, so as to be easily read from the outside. Thomas Mangnall, better known as 'Owd Tummy O'Mangna' received the sum of 1s for the daily conveyance of the letters. A busy man, 'Owd Tummy' also held the positions of rate collector, nuisance inspector, overseer and constable.

James Sharples grocers, No. 64, Market Street, c. 1900. The first employment exchange was at this shop which opened in 1911. It closed in 1914, as there was no unemployment due to the war, and after the war the exchange moved to a place in Church Street. However with the slump there were large dole queues and the Congregational School at the junction of Park Road was used from 1923-1971. In 1971 it moved to a new building in Market Street.

James Sharples, c. 1912. The queue could possibly be as a result of the buildings use as an employment exchange, but it could also be a queue for items in short supply. The women are wearing shawls. Bolton author Bill Naughton, noting in the 1930s that shawls seemed to be going out of fashion, wrote 'a shawl was the most lovely thing any woman could wear – as soft and as comforting as the sound of the word itself. Deep within me, almost like some instinct, was a memory of the warm and comforting wool smell of my mother's shawl, for under that old shawl I must have been carried for many an hour; during the illnesses of childhood, when I was restless, she only had to cover me with her shawl, and the ancient smell of wool and of mother, would calm and console me, so that I would soon slide into a peaceful sleep. A shawl was the most essential garment in homes such as our own, for whatever else a family lacked, no mother was without her shawl.' (Bill Naughton. *Neither Use Nor Ornament*. Bloodaxe Books. 1995.)

106

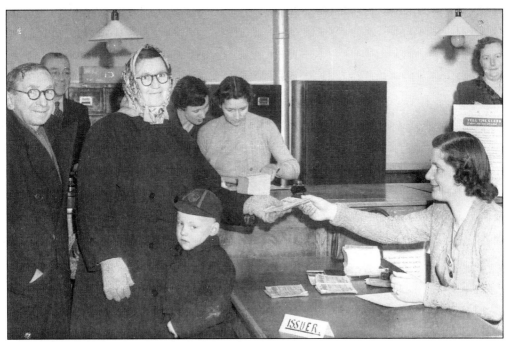

Employment Exchange, Monday 16 April 1951. Mrs Rothwell of No. 15 George Street, received the first of 15,000 ration books to be distributed during April and May, 17% being issued in the first two days, more than any other of the 14 areas in Bolton. Rationing was first introduced in 1941. The rationing of many goods (clothing, furniture, petrol, soap, and certain foodstuffs) had ended by 1950 but the rationing of the main foodstuffs continued until the mid 1950s. A feature of the *Journal* was the 'queue of the week', which in November 1947 was for fireworks.

Number 58 Market Street, 1895, and the Miss Coops are standing outside their shop on the corner of Queen Street.

Advertisement, 1897.

Market Street, 1903-1904, looking towards the Town Hall, which was then under construction. Market Street was called Wade Lane, but this was not considered imposing enough for the address of the civic offices. For years afterwards the stretch from the White Lion retained the old name, until it became Park Road.

Parrs Bank, Market Street, 1900. The bank was built about 1887, and was known as the London County and Westminster and Parrs Bank in 1921, becoming the Westminster in 1925. It is now a bookmakers.

An accident outside Beardsworth hairdressers in Market Street, February 1947. A hairdressers shop was first established at No. 105 Market Street by Elijah Beardsworth in 1882, later moving to No. 31. John Beardsworth was the last to work from this shop, retiring in May 1970, as the shop was due to be demolished. His grandma and grandad, Elijah, were both hairdressers, and his paternal great-grandmother made wigs for Henry Irving. Elijah set a shaving record in 1889 shaving seventy men in thirty-six and a half minutes. John's grandma helped convict a murderer by identifying hair in the murdered girl's hand as coming from the killer's moustache. The shop passed to John's uncle, and continued to be a family business with his aunts also working there. His father then took over in 1921, and kept the shop going through 'thick and thin', – not hair but through strikes, depressions and slumps. John worked as a miner, and part-time in the shop, taking over in 1950. When he retired, an eighty-eight year era of hairdressing by the Beardsworth family in Westhoughton came to an end.

Market Street, in the late 1920s. The shop on the extreme right is that of Mr Billy Holt, plumber and ironmonger. Behind can be seen the veranda fronting the Empire cinema, where patrons could shelter as they queued for the second house. On the left is Ted Partington's old shop, with its cottage window, and cycle tyres hanging by the door. The first electric tram in Westhoughton was on 19 December 1924. The new track went from Deane to the Westhoughton terminus and was 3 miles 21 yards long. (photograph courtesy of Lois Basnett)

Market Street, Bolton, in the late 1940s. Councillors were confident that the tram link would be the beginning of a beautiful friendship. The first car ran at 9.00 a.m. to Westhoughton and back as part of the official inspection. The next car left Bolton at 3 p.m. carrying members of Bolton Tramways and Bolton Council. At the boundary, members of Westhoughton Council joined the tram on its journey to the Westhoughton terminus, where the opening ceremony took place, followed by tea in the Town Hall.

The terminus, November 1946, during the last week of service. At the official opening ceremony, the Mayor of Bolton had said 'he was afraid that the people of Westhoughton and Bolton had in the past looked upon each other as foreigners. One result of today was that it would help them realise they belonged to the same community. It would help them to get to know one another better, so that if future difficulties arose, the greater friendliness assisted by the tram would make the solution simpler. Westhoughton Council had opened their arms to Bolton, and Bolton would not be backward in accepting the embrace.' The sentiments were true but Westhoughton hung on to its independence for as long as possible. In the evening Westhoughton Council were entertained to dinner at the Swan Hotel by the Bolton Tramways Committee. The last tram ran on Sunday, 3 November 1946.

Old Sirs, Daisy Hill, 1935. Five cottages at Old Sirs had to be demolished despite the protest of the owner who said he was prepared to do certain repairs but not raise the roofs. The first list of names, dated 1350, contained the names of John Le Sire and Richard Le Sire, which may have been the origin of the name of the district. Old Sirs was for generations linked with the Green family. At Old Sirs were three of the best orchards in Lancashire, kept by George Green. In 1787 George Green, fustian manufacturers of Westhoughton, had offices in Cross Street, Manchester. From the same family we get Green Fold and Green Common, both in this part of Westhoughton. Daisy Hill Football Club's ground is called New Sirs.

Walter Hibbert and his sister, Margaret Anne, who lived at Lee Hall Farm, Park Road, in the 1890s (Mr W. Hibbert, son of Walter)

Park Road, 1935.

An accident at Park Road, Chequerbent, on 1 July 1953. The footpath was stained with blackcurrant juice when this lorry carrying fruit from Smithfield Market to Wigan crashed into the garden wall of No. 312 Park Road, when the steering gear went wrong on the hill down from Chequerbent. The driver, H.V. Shepherd of Wigan and his companion Donald Crook, escaped uninjured.(photograph courtesy of *Horwich and Westhoughton Journal*)

Park Road, 1940. The road was closed for four days after snow fell heavily on the night of 26 January 1940, one of the worst snowfalls in the last century. Five tramcars were stuck on Snydale Brow and all transport services were cancelled, causing the biggest traffic hold up of all time in Westhoughton. A group of dance band players abandoned their vehicle and walked to the Carnegie Hall where they were due to play at the Cricket Club Dance. Council staff struggled all night to keep roads passable until 8 p.m. on Sunday, when in the words of the foreman, 'they were jiggered up'. On Monday, men were unable to travel out of Westhoughton to work, and had to register at the Employment Exchange. Trains were also affected and one train from Liverpool was stuck on Saturday at Westhoughton for five hours. It contained members of the Arcadian Follies Troupe due to appear at the Bolton Hippodrome. They didn't get out and walk, and the station master's wife provided them with a pot of tea and sandwiches.

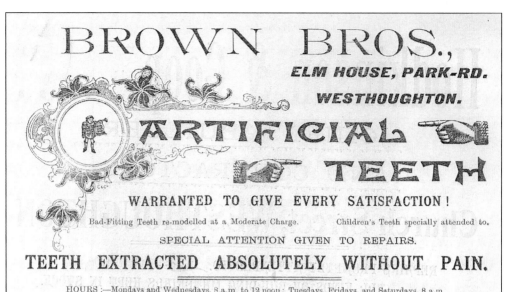

Advertisement, Brown Bros., *c.* 1897

The Grove, Wigan Road, 1905. Mr James Tonge and family. Occupants of the Grove were Ralph Leech, Warden of Westhoughton Chapel (1816), Alice Caldwell (1861), George Caldwell, colliery proprietor and Mrs John Whittaker (1896). James Tonge was a mining engineer from a famous family of engineers connected with Westhoughton.

Nine

Places

From Chequerbent to the White Horse

The Stag and Griffin – this had to make way for the Chequerbent roundabout. One explanation of the name Chequerbent, is that 'bent' means field, and the area was one of chequered fields. Chequerbent though was a mining village, and owed its existence to the many shafts in the area.

The pub, *c.* 1900. The Stag and Griffin was the social centre of the area and overlooked Chequerbent's park, which was little more than a streak of greenery. The Bolton to Leigh railway, the first public railway in Lancashire, ran from Crook Street through Chequerbent, crossing Manchester Road at Hope Cottage. The engineer was George Stephenson, and he stayed at Hulton Hall for three months, as the guest of William Hulton who was chairman of the railway committee. The railway was opened as far as Mr Hulton's collieries on 1 August 1828, and the engine pulling the first train was named '*the Lancashire Witch*'. The Hulton family were benefactors of the district for many years, and their importance was reflected in the title of the station, which used to say, Chequerbent for Hulton Park.

The sale of contents of Hulton Hall, 18 November 1947. The Hall had not been in regular use since 1918, when the late Sir William Hulton moved his home to Cheltenham, where the best pieces were also taken. The sale lasted three days, and among the items described in the catalogue were 'the brass whistle and name plates of the early steam engine Witch'. These raised the sum of £8. Personal effects, furniture, china, and paintings were sold, the first day's sale realising £3,500. A suite of eleven mahogany Chippendale chairs with seats in crimson Morocco leather sold for £550. In its heyday the Hall was a centre of social activity with garden parties and shooting parties. Sir William was succeeded by Sir Roger, who despite having polio, was the senior solicitor to Lancashire Council. He took his own life in 1956, and he was succeeded by Sir Geoffrey.

Sir Geoffrey Hulton is on the extreme left with other judges and officials of the Westhoughton Ploughing and Hedging competitions, in December 1952. Second left, is Ralph Harrison, and third left, Len Holt. In 1958, Hulton Hall was dismantled because it was beyond repair. Sir Geoffrey lived in the house on the Manchester Road side of Hulton Park, allowing the park to be used by the scout movement. When he died there was no heir to the baronetcy.

Chequerbent Mission or Chequerbent Mission church and School, on the Coronation of George VI, May 1937. The mission itself dates back to 1888, the foundation stone being laid by Mrs Hulton, later Lady Hulton.

Daisy Hill School, Standard III, early 1900 (photograph courtesy of Mrs Naylor)

Daisy Hill Station, *c.* 1887. Railway construction, with Leopold the engine, and a 'mechanical navvy'. The station was opened in 1887. In the background you can see a mill on the left, on spare land between Mabel Street and the railway. This was the doubling mill in Leigh Road, worked by Mr Stephen Braddock, The house on the right was a public house, before the Rose and Crown. The stationmaster was Mr Tudge.

Daisy Hill Football Club dance at the Carnegie Hall, 1934.

Daisy Hill Coop, prior to 1914. The shop is advertising the Gala and Sports which was revived after the war, in 1923. It was organized by the Westhoughton Joint Friendly Societies. The gala always had a first rate sports programme, organized to a high standard, according to AAA rules. Arthur Farrimond was a Westhoughton athlete who represented England at the Olympics. He won his first prize for running at the Westhoughton Gala Sports in 1910 when he was seventeen. In 1914 he enlisted in the Ninth Royal Scots, and served on the Western Front and was wounded. After the war when he has recovered from his wounds, he continued his athletic career with Leigh Harriers, eventually turning his attention to fell racing and long distance running. He won the Sporting Chronicle trials race in 1924, and was selected for the English team at the Paris Olympics of 1924, competing in the marathon. Unfortunately, in the closing stages, a spectator ran into the road, collided with him, and brought him down heavily. By the time he regained his stride, seven runners had passed him and he came seventeenth. His commemorative medal is on display in Westhoughton Library. He died on 14 November 1978.

Milk Delivery at Daisy Hill by Mr H. Holden and his sister Polly.

Primitive Methodist Chapel, Daisy Hill, 1902. The Chapel's history began in 1837, when John and Joseph Aspinall became converted to 'Primitive Methodism'. One of them opened his home to a congregation of twenty men and women, but eventually it became necessary to have a building in which to worship. A plot of land for the first chapel was bought from a local nail maker for 1½d per square yard and the chapel was built. The congregation grew and eventually a new church was needed. The chapel, also known as 'T'Ranters' in Hindley Road was built in 1877, and the old church was used to house the Sunday School. It closed in 1985, after cracks were discovered in the structure, and was demolished shortly afterwards. Two houses now stand on the site.

Members of the Church at a field day in the same year. About that time the average congregation was about 100 and there were 140 children being taught in the Sunday School. One of the first ministers was the Revd Samuel Tillotson, who walked from Sowerby Bridge with his family to take up his appointment. His eldest son John was apprenticed to a local printer and he married one of his boss's daughters. John Tillotson was the founder of the evening paper – the *Bolton Evening News*.

Hilton House was a thriving community in 1937 when Miss Mary Pilkington of Hilton House, was crowned by George Formby. Mrs Formby is on his left and behind Mary is Mrs Annie Lowe of the Westhoughton Sick Nursing Association. The attendants are Miss Betty Ratcliffe, (on the right of the Queen), and behind George Formby, is Miss Annie Birtles (later Mrs Roberts of Broadgate Farm, Lostock). (photograph courtesy of *Horwich and Westhoughton Journal*)

Roundthorn, *c.* 1902, near the corner of Miry Lane and France Street. The occupier listed in the 1841 census is Thomas Hampson, silk weaver, aged fifty-five. Marie and Martha Hampson, twin sisters, were born in June 1822 at Roundthorn and lived in the house all their lives. They were never married, never saw the sea, and never travelled on a train. They earned their livelihood by handloom weaving, and lived in the humblest way. Martha died aged eight-two, and Mary aged eighty-five. They were known as the Roundthorn octogenarian twins. When Mary died in February 1908, *the Westhoughton Recorder* produced a postcard photograph of them, with particulars of their life and death, price one penny each.

Westhoughton Chapel. The church or chapel definitely existed before 1500, but the earliest date for a church on the site is not exactly known. There is mention in the Charters of Cockersand Abbey of 'Priest's Croft' around 1200, which was situated in what is now the churchyard and the cemetery, and this suggests that there was a chapel on the site. Very little is known of the early chapel, although in the seventeenth century it was said to be 'thatched'. It was rebuilt and consecrated in 1731. The Hultons at this period were taking quite an active interest in chapel affairs, in spite of their association with Deane, and Mrs Hulton gave the sundial to set off the new chapel, and this is now in the old churchyard. The small building on the extreme right is the original Free School, opened in 1739, and demolished in 1860. The area it occupied was sold to the Local Board for use as a cemetery. It was replaced by the Parochial School in School Street which was opened on 31 May 1860, with accommodation for 280 boys and 140 girls.

The Parochial School, new nursery department, January 1931. The headmistress, near the door, is Miss Leyland and the teacher is Mrs Greenhalgh. The children include Annie Burton, Nellie Rigby, Nellie Halliwell, Doris Hall, Sally Seddon, Elsie Howard, Betty Ratcliffe, Jack Higson, George Hilton, Vera Beardsworth, Lucy Powell, Dorothy Edwards, Allan Gerrard, Marian Crompton, and Doris Booth.

St Bartholomews. In 1867 Westhoughton became a separate parish from Deane, and Mr John Seddon, a local industrialist, said that he would rebuild Westhoughton church. The new church consecrated on St Bartholomew's Day, 1870. The first vicar, the Revd Kinton Jacques, was the incumbent until 1889, and this was a period of phenomenal growth, with a new church at Daisy Hill, schools at Hart Common and Chequerbent, and the establishment of night classes for adults. The vicar became involved in the local government, agitating for a better water supply, and also encouraged sport, particularly Westhoughton Cricket Club. The church was almost totally destroyed by fire on 28 November 1990, with only the tower remaining intact. It was rebuilt, and consecrated on 28 October 1995. Read more in *A Short History of St Bartholomew's Church, Westhoughton* by Robert Walmsley. Revised, 1995.

Saint Bartholomew's old vicarage, which was the home for twenty-nine years of Westhoughton's longest serving vicar, The Revd George Henry St Patrick Garrett. He came to Westhoughton from Horwich, and was vicar from 1908-1937. It was built at three different periods and the oldest portion, surrounding the entrance porch was reputed to be 400 years old. Bishop Gastrell's Notitia Cestriensis – a survey of the old Diocese of Chester made in 1714, stated that 'Westhoughton possessed a good house for ye curate.' The postcard was sent to Mrs Finnigan of No. 145 Church Street, and was dated 4 September 1905.

Garden Party in the vicarage, c. 1935. Canon Garrett is seated in front of the house with Mr and Mrs Howarth next to him. Canon was the last Westhoughton parson to reside in the old vicarage, and he died there in January 1937. A memorial window dedicated to his memory has been installed in the north aisle of the church. The house was condemned and a 'temporary vicarage' in King Street was occupied until the new vicarage was opened in 1939.

Snydale, September 1972. Just over the ridge of Snydale Hill, stood Snydale Hall, a tall and ancient house, at one time five storeys high, which was demolished in 1935. After 500 years of occupation by the Pendlebury and Worthington families, in the mid eighteenth century the house and estate passed into the possession of the Starkies of Huntroyd. In 1807, the following advertisement appeared – 'To be let by ticket at the Nags Head Inn, Bolton at 3 o'clock on the afternoons of 14 and 15 January 1807. Capital messuage and tenements known as Snidle Hall in Westhoughton, consisting of dwelling house, cottage, outhousing, and fifty-eight Cheshire acres of arable land in occupation of James Markland or his under tenants.' The house was reputed to be haunted by the ghost of 'Old Worthington', the last of the line and an arrant spendthrift who hung himself because of his debts. The ghost was truly feared, and was claimed to be the cause of many strange and uncanny happenings around the farm. 'Old Worthington' became so troublesome that the Vicar of Deane was asked to exercise his powers and lay the ghost to rest.

Trinity Methodist church, formerly Wesleyan, c. 1920. Stotts Pit is in the background. John Wesley used the stone as a platform when he preached at Barnaby's Farm, Wimberry Hill, Wingates on 5 April 1785. He had visited Wingates the year before on 16 April 1784, and he recorded in his journal, 'I preached about ten at Win-yate. I was constrained by the multitude of people to preach abroad, though the day was exceedingly cold.' After giving his text, 'all things are ready: come unto the marriage', he adds the remark, 'truly the people were ready too, they drank in every word.' The church was demolished in 1963 and the stone was preserved and now stands in the grounds of Wigan Road Methodist Chapel.

Grove Lane Chapel, *c*. 1900. now Wigan Road Methodist Chapel, though it is still referred to by its original name. Grove Lane became Wigan Road in 1877.

Westhoughton Hall, *c*. 1900, viewed from the south east. The Hall was built by Henry Molyneux, a clothier, who supplied the cottages with wool (later cotton) to be spun, and yarn to be woven. His son Nathaniel married Margaret Bootle, whose family became Bootle-Wilbraham, later to be Earls of Lathom, Lords Skelmersdale, hence Molyneux Road, and Wilbraham Street. It was in Daisy Hill and believed to have been the home of Peter Rylands who fought on the side of Parliament during the civil war, and was taken prisoner at the Battle of Westhoughton Common in 1642. From 1792 to 1812 it was the home of Mr R.J. Lockett, who built the Old Factory. After setting the mill on fire, the rioters also set fire to the Hall, even though he no longer owned the mill. The last tenant, who died in September 1933, was the father of Mrs Williamson, of Hindley Rd., but the owner was Lord Lathom of Ormskirk. In 1948 the council had to ask the last owners, Messrs. T.B. and W. Smith to effect necessary repairs or demolition.

Westhoughton Hall, interior, c. 1907. The door on the left led upstairs and that on the right to the kitchen. The worn step gives some indication of the age of the house. Lord Lathom is said to have removed the carved settle, the two solid black oak doors, and the panelling for his home in Ormskirk, Lathom House. Some of the other items were distributed as follows. Mrs Williamson's daughter had the sideboard, the grandfather clock went to a friend at Daisy Hill, the shells on the sideboard went in Mrs Williamsons garden, the Chippendale mirror was sold to an antique dealer, and the stuffed birds, which were all caught in the grounds, were given to Daisy Hill School. (photograph courtesy of Brian Clare)

White Horse, 25 May 1951. An accident at the White Horse, on the corner of Bolton Road and Manchester Road. A load of steel angle iron forced its way through the cab after a collision with a bus. The White Horse district takes its name from the White Horse Pub. Opposite the inn was a grocery shop kept by George Hunt, who also sold gunpowder to coalminers, for use at the coalface. Tragedy ensued when a match was accidentally dropped into one of the barrels that the powder came in, killing Mrs Hunt in the explosion and injuring the three children.

White Horse Junction, showing the old chip shop and rebuilt corner – the result of several accidents.

The Little Wooden Hut, at Four Lane Ends. The postcard is dated 1923, and was addressed to Rebecca Graham, of No. 5 Waterton Avenue, Blackpool. It was sent by Nellie and Tom, and the message says, 'Willie and John are on the porch. The shop was a newsagent, and in 1912, was owned by a Mr Rushton. Next door to the shop was a tram shelter, and behind it was the old St Andrew's School at Four Lane Ends. The area is named because it is the junction of Salford Road, Manchester Road, New Brook Road and St Helens Road. The Bolton boundary was five feet from the Hulton Arms, and on St Helens Road, the houses were in Westhoughton and the footpath in Bolton.

Place is steept i history
Un characters abeaund
Foak like me class Howfen
Us bein Holy Graewnd

From *Howfen*, by Brian Clare. Brian was born in Westhoughton and has had a life long interest in local dialect and poetry. He performed regularly at the Red Lion Folk Club, and in 1978 won the Samuel Laycock trophy for his dialect poetry. He has been a town councillor for many years and mayor twice.